AF600403

RELATION OF THE LOCAL ORDINARY TO RELIGIOUS OF DIOCESAN APPROVAL

THE CATHOLIC UNIVERSITY OF AMERICA
CANON LAW STUDIES
No. 283

RELATION OF THE LOCAL ORDINARY TO RELIGIOUS OF DIOCESAN APPROVAL

A HISTORICAL SYNOPSIS AND A COMMENTARY

BY

THE REV. STEPHEN QUINN, M.S.SS.T., J.C.L.
PRIEST OF THE CONGREGATION OF THE MISSIONARY SERVANTS OF THE MOST HOLY TRINITY

A DISSERTATION

SUBMITTED TO THE FACULTY OF THE SCHOOL OF CANON LAW OF THE CATHOLIC UNIVERSITY OF AMERICA IN PARTIAL FULFILLMENT OF THE REQUIREMENTS FOR THE DEGREE OF DOCTOR OF CANON LAW

THE CATHOLIC UNIVERSITY OF AMERICA PRESS
WASHINGTON, D. C.
1949

Imprimi Potest:
THOMAS O'KEEFFE, M.S.SS.T.,
Vicarius
Silver Spring, Md., die 12 octobris, 1948

Nihil Obstat:
HIERONYMUS D. HANNAN, A.M., S.T.D., LL.B., J.C.D.,
Censor Deputatus
Washingtonii, D. C., die 12 octobris, 1948

Imprimatur:
✠ PATRICIUS A. O'BOYLE, D.D.,
Archiepiscopus Washingtoniensis
Washingtonii, die 12 octobris, 1948

PRINTED IN THE UNITED STATES OF AMERICA
MURRAY & HEISTER, INC.—WASHINGTON, D. C.

TO MARY, QUEEN
OF THE
MISSIONARY CENACLE

TABLE OF CONTENTS

PART II

CANONICAL COMMENTARY

FOREWORD

It is essential for the just and efficient government of dioceses as well as of religious institutes that the rights and duties of the local ordinary in relation to these religious institutes be fully determined. Especially true is this in reference to congregations of diocesan approval, inasmuch as such institutes are more extensively subject to the jurisdiction of the local ordinary than are other types of religious institutes, while at the same time these institutes of diocesan approval are autonomous, self-governing, moral persons. It is true that such institutes, especially in the early years of their development, have a need for the guidance and vigilance of the local ordinary. It is necessary, however, for their proper development and for the full realization of their purpose that such institutes enjoy the full exercise of their rights within the law.

The extent of the local ordinary's jurisdiction over congregations of diocesan approval must be measured in the light of their particular status within the framework of the Church. It is therefore the purpose of this work to indicate the nature and extent of the local ordinary's jurisdiction over such institutes in accordance with the laws of the Church which govern the foundation and continued existence of such institutes.

Since congregations of simple vows came into existence only after the Council of Trent, the historical section of this work treats only in a general way the pre-Tridintine history of the relationship between the bishop and the religious within his diocese. For this reason a chronological order is observed in the presentation of the material covering the period from the founding of the religious life up to the Council of Trent. For the period following the Council of Trent up to the Code, a topical arrangement is observed.

The writer wishes to express his sincere gratitude to his religious superiors for the opportunity of graduate study in Canon

Law, to the members of the Faculty of the School of Canon Law for their generous instruction, assistance and guidance, to his brothers and sisters of the Missionary Cenacle for their aid, encouragement and prayer, and to all others who in any way aided in the writing of this work.

CHAPTER I

GENERAL NOTIONS

In order to establish clearly the scope and purpose of this work, it is necessary first to define the terms to be used. Under the term local ordinary are included residential bishops, abbots or prelates *nullius* and the vicars general of these, administrators, vicars and prefects apostolic within their territories as well as those who at the departure of the foregoing from office temporarily succeed them in government according to the provisions of law or of approved constitutions.[1] These possess the public power of ruling or governing within the confines of their territory. This power is known as jurisdiction, and may be defined as a public power granted by Christ or by His Church through a canonical mission, for the governing of the baptized in their aim to reach the goal of eternal life.[2]

By religious congregations of men and women of diocesan approval are understood those congregations, the members of which profess simple vows, and which have not as yet received at least the decree of praise from the Holy See.[3] The internal affairs of such institutes are governed by the superiors and chapters of these institutes according to the norms of the constitutions and the general law.[4] Superiors and chapters govern the institute through the dominative power which they possess over its members.[5] This

---

[1] Canon 198, §§ 1, 2—*Codex Iuris Canonici Pii X Pontificis Maximi iussu digestus Benedicti Papae XV auctoritate promulgatus, Praefatione, Fontium annotatione et Indice Analytico-Alphabetico ab Emo Petro Card. Gasparri Auctus* (Romae: Typis Polyglottis Vaticanis, 1917). Hereafter cited by canons.)

[2] Maroto, *Institutiones Iuris Canonici* (2 vols., Vol. I, 3 ed., Romae, 1919–1921), I, 666.

[3] Canon 487, nn. 2, 3.

[4] Canon 501, § 1.

[5] Canon 501, § 1. "Dominative power comes directly from the act by

dominative power, proper to imperfect societies, is a preceptive power by means of which the ends and purpose of the institute can be attained.[6]

While canon 501, § 1, grants to superiors and chapters of the institute dominative power over its members, canon 492, § 2, fully subjects such institutes of diocesan approval to the jurisdiction of the local ordinary according to the norm of the law. It will therefore be the purpose and scope of this work to determine the extent of the local ordinary's jurisdiction as granted to him by the common law and by particular constitutions, establishing as far as is possible the rights and duties both of the local ordinary and of the institute relative to such matters as the foundation and suppression of the congregation, of the province and of an individual house; canonical visitation; government of the institute; administration of temporal goods; and the admission and departure of candidates.

---

which, in taking the vow of obedience in a community, Christians assume the obligation to work therein within the scope of the institute under the guidance of those members to whom the direction of the society is entrusted by due appointment or election."—Papi, *The Government of Religious Communities* (New York: P. J. Kenedy & Sons, 1919), p. 61.

[6] Raus, *De Sacrae Obedientiae Virtute et Voto* (2 vols., Lugduni: Emmanuel Vitte, 1923), I, 65.

PART I

HISTORICAL SYNOPSIS

SECTION I

RELATION OF BISHOPS TO RELIGIOUS BEFORE THE COUNCIL OF TRENT

CHAPTER II

FROM THE FIRST TO THE THIRTEENTH CENTURY

Article 1. Early Ages of the Church

In examining the relationship which existed between the bishops and religious of the first centuries of the Church, one finds no juridical distinction which separated the religious from the other Christians of that period.[1] This is understandable, since that period was the formative age of both the Church and the religious state. Religious life, with its basis in the invitation of Christ to a higher life,[2] found its first practical application in the lives of the early Christians, especially the virgins and ascetics.[3]

It was only toward the middle of the third century that the religious state had taken on some of the characteristics of that state as it is known at the present time. At that time in Egypt and Asia Minor there existed several organized communities of ascetics and virgins.[4] Still, even with the advent of the complete religious state there was as yet no indication of the relationship that existed between the bishops and the religious within his diocese.[5]

It is known that St. Augustine (+430) followed the practice of obtaining the consent of the bishop of the place before erect-

---

[1] Wernz, *Ius Decretalium ad Usum Praelectionum in Scholis Textus Iuris Canonici, sive Iuris Decretalium* (6 vols., Romae, 1898–1905), III, n. 602 (hereinafter cited *Ius Decretalium*).

[2] Matth., XIX, 29.

[3] Montalembert, *The Monks of the West* (2 vols., translated by Thomas B. Noonan, Boston, 1872), I, 170.

[4] Schäfer, *Compendium de Religiosis ad Normam Codicis Iuris Canonici* (Münster in W.: Ex Officina Libraria Aschendorff, 1927), p. 19 (hereafter cited *De Religiosis*).

[5] Reilly, *The Visitation of Religious,* The Catholic University of America Canon Law Studies, n. 112 (Washington, D. C.: The Catholic University of America, 1938), pp. 31–32.

ing a new monastery.[6] There was also the case of Martin of Tours (+397) who "asked permission of the Bishop of Potiers in 360 to found a monastery in that city."[7] At the very most, however, there seems to have been required only the tacit approval of the local bishop for the erection of monasteries during that early period.[8]

ARTICLE 2. THE COUNCIL OF CHALCEDON (451)

Following the period of the persecution, when the monks returned from the desert to the urban centers, there arose a need for a clear delineation in the relationship between bishop and religious.[9] This need was accentuated by the heresy of Eutychianism, which caused such great harm to the early Church. Eutyches (+ca. 454), himself a monk, had the following of many monks in his disregard for the authority of the bishops.[10]

Thus it was that the Council of Chalcedon, convoked for the purpose of combating the errors of Eutyches, instituted the first general legislation for religious. No new monasteries were to be built or erected without the permission of the local ordinary, and those already built were to be under the authority of the bishop, as also the clergy and the monks in them. Disregard of these rules meant canonical penalties for the clerics, and excommunication for the monks.[11] The permission of the local ordinary became the requirement even for civil recognition, for the canon

---

[6] Orth, *The Approbation of Religious Institutes,* The Catholic University of America Canon Law Studies, n. 71 (Washington, D. C.: The Catholic University of America, 1931), p. 12; Van Espen, *Opera Omnia* (4 vols., Lovanii, 1753), T. I, pars 1, tit. 24, c. 3.

[7] Orth, *The Approbation of Religious Institutes,* p. 12; Montalembert, *The Monks of the West,* I, 340.

[8] Schmalzgrueber, *Ius Ecclesiasticum Universum* (5 vols. in 12, Romae, 1843-1845), lib. III, tit. 36, n. 28; Wernz, *Ius Decretalium,* III, n. 616.

[9] Flanagan, *The Canonical Erection of Religious Houses,* The Catholic University of America Canon Law Studies, n. 179 (Washington, D. C.: The Catholic University of America Press, 1943), p. 2.

[10] Flanagan, *op. cit.,* p. 2.

[11] Mansi, *Sacrorum Conciliorum Nova et Amplissima Collectio* (53 vols. in 60, Parisiis, Arnhem, Lipsiae, 1901–1927), VII, 359–362 (hereafter cited Mansi).

enacted in the Council of Chalcedon became incorporated also in the Justinian Code.[12] For the possession of juridical status the erection of each new monastery needed the consent of the bishop in whose diocese it was erected.[13]

Article 3. Particular Legislation up to the Year 1123

The laws that were passed at the Council of Chalcedon together with the particular legislation that was enacted in the following century and a half had the effect of bringing about the constituting of each monastery as a separate diocesan institute.[14]

In 455 the III Council of Arles enacted the law that lay monks were solely under their abbots, and that bishops could not ordain any of them without the abbot's consent. This legislation arose out of a dispute between Faustus, Abbot of the Monastery in Lerins (433–ca. 460) and Theodore, Bishop of Frejus (433–455).[15] The Council of Agde in 506 repeated the prohibition of the Council of Chalcedon against the founding of new monasteries without the consent of the bishop. On the other hand, the bishop was not to ordain any of the monks without the consent of the abbot.[16]

The I Council of Orleans (511), repeating the foregoing prohibitions, ordered that the bishop of the place should correct abbots who acted beyond their power, and added that the bishops should gather the abbots together in some convenient place each year to determine the conditions prevailing in each monastery.[17] This was

---

[12] *Corpus Iuris Civilis,* Vol. III, *Novellae Constitutiones* (ed. 5. stereotypa, recognovit R. Schoell. Opus Schoelli morte interceptum absolvit G. Kroll, Berolini: Apud Weidmannos, 1928), N. (5.1); (131.7).

[13] Orth, *The Approbation of Religious Institutes,* p. 18.

[14] Reilly, *The Visitation of Religious,* p. 33.

[15] Mansi, VII, 908; Thomassinus, *Vetus et Nova Ecclesiae Disciplina circa Beneficia et Beneficiarios* (3 vols., Venetiis, 1730), Pars I, lib. III, cap. 26, n. 16 (hereafter cited *Vetus et Nova Ecclesiae Disciplina*).

[16] " Monasterium novum, nisi episcopo, aut permittente, aut probante, nullus incipere, aut fundare praesumat. . . . Si necesse fuerit clericum de monachis ordinari, cum consensu et voluntate abbatis praesumat episcopus."—Mansi, VIII, 329.

[17] Canon 19: " Abbates pro humilitate religionis in episcoporum potestate consistant; et si quid extra regulam fecerint, ab episcopo corrigantur: qui semel in anno, in loco ubi episcopus elegerit, accepta vocatione, conveniant.

but a further determination of the general norm enacted in the Council of Chalcedon, namely, that all monasteries were subject to the bishop. In 517 the Council of Epaon strengthened the bishop's power by granting him the authority to remove delinquent abbots from office, but there was reserved for the abbot the right of appeal to the metropolitan.[18]

This right of the bishop's act of visitation and of his removal of delinquent abbots from their offices was fundamental in the question of the subjection of religious to the local bishop. It will be seen that this was a right which the bishops were reluctant to relinquish. Thus in the one case of papal exemption known at that time, namely, that granted by Pope Hormisdas (514–523) to the monastery of women founded by St. Caesarius of Arles (470–542), provision was made for an occasional visitation of the monastery by the Bishop of Arles.[19]

In Africa monasteries seemed to enjoy a greater degree of freedom from the local ordinary's jurisdiction. In the Council of Carthage (525) Abbot Peter of the province of Byzacena in a dispute with the bishop argued for the preservation of this traditional freedom from the authority of the bishops as it had been accorded to the monks in Africa.[20] In Spain, however, the Council of Barcelona (ca. 540) reaffirmed the teaching of the Council of Chalcedon,[21] while in France the II Council of Orleans (533) took over from the Council of Epaon (517) canon 19, which granted to bishops the right to punish and remove delinquent abbots, but reserved the right of appeal for the abbot in the case

---

Monachi autem abbatibus omni se obedientiae devotione subiiciant." Mansi, VIII, 354.

[18] *Monumenta Germaniae Historica, Leges in 4o,* Sectio III (Concilia), Tom. I (ed. F. Maassen, Hanoverae, 1893), 24 (hereafter cited *MGH*).

[19] It is to be noted, however, that this was not a monastery under an abbot. Cf. Jaffé, *Regesta Pontificum Romanorum ab condita Ecclesia ad annum post Christum natum MCXCVIII,* editionem secundam correctam et auctam auspiciis Wattenbach, curaverunt S. Löwenfeld, F. Kaltenbrunner, P. Ewald (2 vols. in 1, Lipsiae, 1885–1888), n. 864 (hereafter cited Jaffé).

[20] Reilly, *The Visitation of Religious,* pp. 34–35; Thomassinus, *Vetus et Nova Ecclesiae Disciplina,* Pars I, lib. III, cap. 31, n. 9.

[21] Mansi, IX, 110.

of removal.[22] The V Council of Arles (554) placed the responsibility for the discipline of the monasteries upon the local bishop.[23]

The West from the sixth century onward made great advances in the development of the monastic life, principally through the original and influential contribution of St. Benedict (480–c. 547). The monasticism of the East had already begun to reveal a decline, which was due in some measure to the heretical tendency of the monks and the continued persecution to which they were subjected by the Byzantine Empire.[24]

With the coming of St. Benedict and his rule, there came also greater unity, coherence and stability in monasticism. Benedict's rule, publicly praised by Gregory the Great (590–604) in 595 at the Council of Rome, had as its keynote a life in common under the paternal guidance of the abbot, and was so ideally suited for the religious life that it became eventually the code of all monastic institutions for many years to come.[25] Concomitant with this rebirth of the monastic ideal came a sharper delineation in the relationship between bishops and religious, greater consideration being shown for the monasteries and their rights. This policy had its origin with the Holy See, especially under Gregory the Great (590–604), who valued greatly the work of the monasteries.[26] Gregory expressly forbade all unnecessary interference on the part of bishops with the affairs of the monasteries, since this only destroyed good order and proper discipline. At the same time, however, he did not destroy the right and duty of the bishops to visit at the proper time and in the proper manner the various monasteries within his diocese. In fact he reproved those bishops who failed in their duty here.[27]

---

[22] Can. 21—*MGH, Leges,* Sectio III, I, 64.

[23] C. 5—*MGH, Leges,* Sectio III, I, 119.

[24] Montalembert, *Monks of the West,* I, 219; Farrell, *The Rights and Duties of the Local Ordinary Regarding Women Religious of Pontifical Approval,* The Catholic University of America Canon Law Studies, n. 128 (Washington, D. C.: The Catholic University of America Press, 1941), p. 14.

[25] Augustine, *A Commentary on the New Code of Canon Law* (8 vols., B. Herder Co., St. Louis, Vol. III, 5. ed., 1938), III, 7.

[26] Gallik, *The Rights and Duties of Bishops Regarding Diocesan Sisterhoods* (St. Paul, Minn.: Wanderer Publishing Co., 1939), p. 6.

[27] Reilly, *The Visitation of Religious,* p. 38; *Monumenta Germaniae His-*

The Provincial Council of Seville (619)[28] and the XVII Provincial Council of Toledo (694)[29] repeated the previous legislation concerning the necessity of obtaining the bishop's permission for the erection of new monasteries. In the so-called "*Excerptiones*" of Egbert of York (735–766) the bishops were commanded to correct delinquent abbots and to convene them once a year at some designated place with a view to determining the conditions existing in the monasteries.[30]

Paschal II (1099–1118) in a letter to the Bishop of Bologna revealed the fact that monks and abbots in their parishes had assumed the episcopal rights and offices without the permission of the bishop or the authority of the Apostolic See. This militated against the canons of the Council of Chalcedon, and Paschal ordered an end to such assumption of power without the proper permission of the bishop or of the Apostolic See itself.[31]

From a consideration of the legislation subsequent to the Council of Chalcedon (451) it is evident aside from the matter of exemptions and privileges, which are treated later in Chapter VI, that each monastery was dependent upon the local ordinary for its juridical personality, and was completely subject to him in the maintenance of discipline and the true monastic spirit.[32]

Article 4. The I Lateran Council (1123)

In the I Lateran Council, canon seventeen reflected an abuse practiced by the monks, namely of taking over the care of souls

torica, Gregorii I Papae registrum epistolarum (Tom. I, pars I, libri i–iv, edidit Paulus Ewald, 1887; Tom. I, pars II, libri v–vii, post Pauli Ewaldi obitum, edidit L. M. Hartmann, 1889; Tom. II, libri viii–xiv, post Pauli Ewaldi obitum, edidit L. M. Hartmann, 1893–1899), *Ep. I,* v. 49; *Ep. II,* viii, 17; *Ep. I,* vi, 28; *Ep. I,* vii, 12.

[28] C. 10—Mansi, X, 655.

[29] C. 11—Mansi, XII, 106.

[30] Cc. 62, 63—Mansi, XII, 419.

[31] Mansi, XX, 1073.

[32] Justinian law reflected this dependence of monasteries on their bishops. The Emperor approved the Council of Chalcedon and the pertinent canons were incorporated into the Code and Novels. Cf. C (1.3); (22.2); (43.5); 46.3); N. (123.36, 42); N. 59; N. (79.1). Justinian law laid particular stress on the bishop's obligation of visitation and correction, making the superior of each monastery directly responsible to the bishop. Cf. C. (1.3) 39.

outside the monastery without the due permission of the bishop, and of usurping and appropriating certain episcopal rights and privileges.[33] For in canon seventeen it was forbidden to abbots and monks to impose public penances, to visit the sick, to administer the sacrament of extreme unction, and to sing public masses. And in such matters as concerned the obtaining of the chrism and the holy oils, and also the procuring of the consecration of altars and the ordination of clerics, abbots were referred to the bishops in whose diocese they resided.[34]

Thus this Council, in legislating for the entire Church, asserted the complete jurisdiction of the bishops over the subjects within their territory. To the bishop alone belonged the right and the duty to care for the spiritual needs of those within his diocese. Monasteries had no right to take to themselves any of these rights or privileges. In such cases in which the religious did not hold their church "*pleno iure,*" they had to present the priests destined for service in that church to the bishop for his approval. The priest then was responsible to the bishop in his work for the care of souls in that parish.[35]

Article 5. The "Decretum" of Gratian (ca. 1140)

In Gratian's *Decretum* there was collected together much of the legislation that first found expression in the Council of Chalcedon (451) and in the particular councils celebrated in later centuries. In some cases there was also a further presentation, inasmuch as Gratian added his own *dicta* on the various canons. Thus Gratian, in adverting to the prohibition which barred the erection of monasteries without the proper permission of the bishop,[36] noted in his *dicta* to this canon that the clerics of each monastery were under the power of the bishop, and as such were subject to him in the building of any new monasteries.

Those who chose the monastic life were to subject themselves

---

[33] Schroeder, *Disciplinary Decrees of the General Councils* (St. Louis, Mo., B. Herder Co., 1937), p. 190 (hereafter cited *Disciplinary Decrees*).

[34] Mansi, XXI, 285.

[35] Schroeder, *Disciplinary Decrees,* p. 223.

[36] From the Council of Chalcedon—c. 10, C. XVIII, q. 2.

to their bishops, and to give themselves over to a life of prayer, fasting and work. Once having entered the monasteries, they were not to leave them save for an urgent necessity and at the command of the bishop.[37] Gratian, in his comment, pointed out the fact that the law prohibited the departure of the monks from the monastery for the performance of any of the priestly functions, such as the burying of the dead. He stated, however, that this did not prohibit them from burying anyone who had expressed his desire to receive burial within the monastery. In support of this Gratian quoted a letter of Gregory the Great (590–604), written in the year 590, in which the religious were given permission to bury their dead within their own monastery.[38]

In another of his *dicta,* Gratian stated that for various reasons there had been admitted to the monasteries many who failed to observe the discipline, and thus became rather a source of trouble. The obligation rested upon the abbot to correct any such lapses and to rule his monks wisely. Failing in this, he was liable to the bishop for any necessary correction.[39] The bishop in turn had the duty to make a visitation frequently within the year to see to the proper upholding of the discipline of the monastery, and to correct those things which needed correction.[40] The task, however, of visiting and exhorting the religious was to be conducted in a spirit of charity, lest any needless harm befall the monastery.[41]

Gratian further noted in his *dicta* that the monasteries were free from the power and dominion of the bishop in reference to the goods of the monastery, so that he could not convert these to his own use. In support of this doctrine Gratian referred to legislation by Gregory I at the Council of Rome (601).[42] The monks were also free from the power of the bishop in the in-

---

[37] From the Council of Chalcedon—c. 12, C. XVI, q. 1.

[38] From a Letter of Gregory I in the year 590—c. 13, C. XVI, q. 1.

[39] From the II Council of Orleans (533)—c. 15, C. XVIII, q. 2.

[40] From the I Council of Orleans (511)—c. 29, C. XVIII, q. 2.

[41] From a letter of Gregory I written in 597 to the Bishop of Ravenna—c. 28, c. XVIII, q. 2.

[42] C. 5, C. XVIII, q. 2.

ternal rule of the monastery. This was exclusively in the hands of the monks.[43]

The monks could not, however, usurp any episcopal rights, such as the imposing of public penances, the granting of the remission of sins, and the like. These rights were to be assumed by the monks with the consent of the bishop alone.[44] The monks, however, were to be chosen for the office of clerics only upon the testimony of the abbot and with his consent.[45]

From a consideration of the legislation as collected by Gratian and as analyzed in his commentary on it, it is possible to ascertain to some extent the relation that existed between bishops and monks at that time. Fundamental was the right of the local ordinary to approve the erection of new monasteries. Once erected, these monasteries were subject to the bishops under the immediate direction of the abbots. The bishops had the right and the duty to visit these monasteries frequently to see to the maintenance of the proper discipline, but in a manner in harmony with Christian charity. The bishop had however no right to interfere with the internal rule of the monks, for this responsibility fell exclusively to the abbots and the superiors of the monasteries. The bishops likewise were not to ordain priests from the ranks of the monks without the consent of their abbot. Yet, once they were ordained, the monks were to look to the bishop for the necessary permission to exercise any of the episcopal rights.

Article 6. Exemption

While it is true that the conclusions drawn in the previous article represent in general the relationship that then existed between the bishops and religious, nevertheless consideration must be given to the fact that there were exceptions to this complete subjection of the religious to the bishop. It will be necessary therefore to treat briefly the subject of exemption as it affected this relationship.

---

[43] From a letter of Pope Pelagius I, written sometime between 556–561—c. 30, C. XVIII, q. 2.

[44] From a letter of Paschal II (1099–1118) to the Bishop of Bologna—c. 9, C. XVI, q. 1.

[45] From the Council of Agde (506)—c. 33, C. XVI, q. 2.

Pope Gregory the Great (590–604) did not institute exemption, though he did insist on the rights of the monks to elect their own abbot, to take care of the administration of temporalities and to exercise control over the revenues, the property and the documents belonging to the monastery.[46] It is only in a later period that one finds the first indication of monastic exemption. There was first of all an increasing effort on the part of the monasteries both to free themselves from the interference of the bishops in the election of the abbot and to secure their property against outside intermeddling.[47] These objectives were obtained through the granting of charters by the Holy See.[48] Such charters did not, however, entirely deny the bishop's right of visitation and supervision. In the ninth century, as the necessity for them increased, these charters from the Holy See were obtained more frequently.[49] Yet, though papal and royal exemptions had been granted before the eleventh century, it is not possible to say that the monasteries were entirely free of episcopal jurisdiction through the tenth century.[50]

In the eleventh and twelfth centuries the status of monastic exemption gained its full development. The Popes were insistent in their efforts for reform, and had the full backing of such monastic groups as the Cluniacs, the Camaldolese, the Vallumbrosians, the Carthusians and the Cistercians, whose centralized

[46] Augustine, *A Commentary on the New Code of Canon Law,* III, 25.

[47] Thomassinus, *Vetus et Nova Ecclesiae Disciplina,* Pars I, lib. III, cap. 27, nn. 6–12.

[48] Thomassinus, *Vetus et Nova Ecclesiae Disciplina,* Pars I, lib. III, cap. 27, nn. 6–12.

[49] Reilly, *The Visitation of Religious,* p. 49.

[50] Thomassinus, *Vetus et Nova Ecclesiae Disciplina,* Pars I, Lib. III, cap. 32, nn. 9–11. Exceptions were the Monastery of Bobbio, founded in 612 by St. Columban (+615) and obtaining the status of exemption in 628, as well as the Monasteries of Fulda and of Monte Cassino, and two monasteries in Benevento, all of which seem to have obtained a complete release from subjection to the jurisdiction of the local bishops, along with exemption from the episcopal visitation. Cf. *Privilegium Bobiensi Coenbio Datum*—Migne, *Patrologia Cursus Completus, Series Latina* (221 vols., Parisiis, 1844–1864), LXXX, 483 (hereafter cited *MPL*); *Epistola XV Zachariae Papae*—*MPL,* LXXXIX, 944.

government transcended diocesan lines.[51] In consideration of the work these monastic groups were accomplishing for the reform, and with a view to lending them further aid, the Holy See granted them certain immunities from the jurisdiction of the local bishops.[52]

The monks of Cluny, for example, possessed many such immunities, which offered occasion for the Council of Anse (1025) and the Bishop of Mâcon to challenge their validity by pointing to them as contravening the decrees of the fourth canon of the Council of Chalcedon (451), which canon had placed all religious under the jurisdiction of the bishops. But their efforts availed them nothing. Gregory VII (1073–1085), Urban II (1088–1099) and Callistus II (1119–1124) saw fit to share with the religious groups even further concessions.[53]

Two further causes, either canonical or secular in character, gave rise to monastic exemption. The canonical cause originated most probably with the Irish-Scottish Church in its characteristic monastic setup. In this setup the monasteries committed their possessions to the Holy See in return for a charter of exemption. The secular cause had its origin in the fact that for the monasteries which the King founded he granted certain immunities from service rendered in behalf of the administrative needs of the country. This included especially an immunity from the fiscal regulations, inasmuch as royal rights were shared with the monastery. In consequence of this transfer of royal rights there came into prominence a royal official (*advocatus*), whose task it was to administer the royal rights in the name of the monastery. This office later became a benefice. The continued royal favor and control inherent in this arrangement led to the monastery's complete withdrawal from the bishop's jurisdiction.

As a consequence of this kind of exemption the abbots became territorial lords under a system of lay investiture. The established advocacy became an inheritable fief which yielded a set income. But this office became also a tool of exploitation and a source of much suffering. The royal control was strongly felt

[51] Reilly, *The Visitation of Religious*, p. 43.
[52] Reilly, *The Visitation of Religious*, p. 44.
[53] Reilly, *The Visitation of Religious*, p. 44.

in the monasteries. From the tenth century onward monasteries tried to break away from the royal or secular exemption, and instead to obtain a canonical exemption. To achieve this they declared themselves vassals of the Holy See. In that manner there was set up a distinctly new kind of relationship between the bishop and the religious.[54]

It is true that there was a tendency on the part of some monasteries to utilize beyond their intended limits the exemptions that had been gained. The extent of the exemption was not uniform in all the cases. In order to ascertain to what extent any particular group was freed from the authority and jurisdiction of the local ordinary, one had to examine the individual formularies which certified the specific status of exemption.[55]

In greater measure the monastic groups which enjoyed exemptions were those which pertained to religious institutes which possessed a centralized form of government that transcended diocesan lines. Autonomous monasteries were as a rule nonexempt. This was the status of affairs at the end of the twelfth century. Thus it was that the jurisdiction of the bishops over the religious within their dioceses had become considerably limited and circumscribed through the extant juridical fact of exemption.[56]

---

[54] Reilly, *The Visitation of Religious,* p. 43.

[55] Augustine, *A Commentary on the New Code of Canon Law,* III, 31. Augustine noted that there were three types of religious bodies: (1) Those who were not free at all from the jurisdiction of the bishop, since they possessed no papal brief; (2) those who had a limited protection, but were in some degree still subject to the local ordinary; (3) those who were under the special tutelage of the Apostolic See, and hence were free from the coercive power of the local bishop. Cf. Augustine, *op. cit.,* III, 32.

[56] Reilly, *The Visitation of Religious,* p. 42.

CHAPTER III

FROM THE THIRTEENTH CENTURY TO THE COUNCIL OF TRENT (1545–1563)

ARTICLE 1. FROM THE IV COUNCIL OF THE LATERAN (1215) TO BONIFACE VIII (1294–1303)

Deeply concerned with the welfare of the Church, Innocent III (1198–1216) in the Council he convoked in 1215 (the IV General Council of the Lateran) made the first great change since the Council of Chalcedon (451) in the method of approval for religious institutes. The reason for the pope's concern was the ever increasing number of orders then being established in the Church. The resultant confusion together with the tendency which some of them had towards heresy, as also the great burden that it became to support them, led Innocent to decree in canon 13 of this Council that no new orders were to be founded, and that anyone who wished to enter an order was to choose one already established. Anyone who desired to found a new monastery had to adopt for the new monastery a rule that was already approved.[1]

The immediate provocation for this law was the heretical sect of the Waldensians. This sect, founded by Waldo about the year 1176, professed such errors as the rejection of purgatory, the repudiation of all oaths and the disclaiming of indulgences. Condemned by Alexander III (1159–1181) and later by Lucius III (1181–1185) they nevertheless continued to exist, and even demanded of Innocent III his approval of their way of life. Innocent saw in this sect a great danger. He sensed the need of a

[1] Canon 13: " Ne nimia religionum diversitas gravem in Ecclesia Dei confusionem inducat, firmiter prohibemus ne quis de cetero novam religionem inveniat; sed quicumque voluerit ad religionem converti, unam de approbatis assumat. Similiter qui voluerit religiosam domum fundare de novo, regulam et institutionem accipiat de religionibus approbatis." C. 9, X, *de religiosis domibus,* III, 36; Schroeder, *Disciplinary Decrees,* p. 255.

stronger power than that of the bishops for regulating the religious life, in order to guard against the springing up of similar sects that would profess a false way of perfection. Once established, these sects could cause grave difficulty to the Church.[2] The conciliar enactment in effect required a formal approval from the Holy See for any new institutes. St. Dominic (1170–1221) adopted the rule of St. Augustine, and his order was approved by the Holy See as were the orders of the Franciscans, the Augustinians and the Carmelites.[3]

But the efforts of Innocent did not meet with any great success, for mendicant orders did come into existence after this council without the required approval. This was the condition of things when in 1274 Gregory X at the II General Council of Lyons in the twenty-third canon abolished all orders that had come into existence after 1215 without the proper approval of the Holy See.[4]

By the action of the IV Lateran Council (1215) the right of approving religious orders was taken from the local ordinaries and reserved exclusively to the Holy See. Thus there was set aside the legislation of the Council of Chalcedon on this matter. In point of fact, however, the new provision made in the law was not always observed, nor did later legislation confirm it.[5] Contrary custom instead obtained the force of law. Accordingly there were repeated instances in which religious institutes were erected solely with the permission of the local ordinary.[6]

Particular legislation subsequent to the IV Lateran Council reiterated the bishop's duty of visitation.[7] The trend however

---

[2] Suarez, *Opera Omnia* (26 vols., Parisiis, 1856-1861), T. III, lib. II, c. 15, n. 15; Orth, *The Approbation of Religious Institutes,* p. 29.

[3] Schäfer, *De Religiosis,* n. 64.

[4] Mansi, XXIV, 96–97.

[5] Bouix, *Tractatus de Jure Regularium* (3. ed., 3 vols., Parisiis, 1882–1883), I, 213 (hereafter cited *De Jure Regularium*).

[6] Farrell, *The Rights and Duties of the Local Ordinary Regarding Women Religious of Pontifical Right,* p. 19; Bouix, *De Jure Regularium,* I, 210.

[7] German National Council (1287), c. 27—Hefele, *Conciliengeschichte* (9 vols., Freiburg im Br., Herder, Vols. I–VI, 2. ed. 1873–1890; Vols. VII–IX, 1. ed. 1887–1890), VI, 249; Council of Aquileia (1339), c. 1—Hefele, *op. cit.,* VI, 647; Council of Padua (1350), c. 20—Hefele, *op. cit.,* VI, 695;

was away from the subjection to the bishop which was implied in his right of visitation. In the thirteenth century especially the monastic exemptions were widened to an extent that included not only a freedom from the episcopal visitation, but also an immunity from the penal authority of the bishops. This in effect rendered nugatory whatever power of jurisdiction the bishops enjoyed over those who possessed such exemptions.[8]

ARTICLE 2. FROM BONIFACE VIII TO THE V COUNCIL OF THE LATERAN (1512–1517)

Boniface VIII (1294–1303) tried to halt this trend. Through his Constitution *Periculoso* in 1298 he did succeed in legislating special requirements for nuns. The nuns were to observe a strict enclosure. They could leave the monastery only in the case of a grave sickness which involved danger for the health of the others in the monastery. None was to enter the monastery except for a reasonable cause, and then only with the permission of the proper superior. It was the duty of the bishops to uphold the observance of this law, even in monasteries of nuns subject directly to the Holy See.[9] This regulation along with the duties entailed by it for the bishops was made more specific in 1312, when Clement V (1305–1314) in his Constitution *Attendentes* ordered the bishops to visit annually the monasteries of nuns, inclusive not only of those which were subject to them, but also of those which were subject directly to the Holy See.[10]

The Council of Constance (1414–1418) achieved some measure of success in its efforts to curb at least some of the privileges granted to regulars during the period of the Great Schism (1378–1417),[11] but with Sixtus IV (1471–1484) the religious orders gained further advances in freeing themselves from the authority

Council of Rheims (1408)—Mansi, XXVI, 1068–1076; Council of Cologne (1452), c. 16—Hefele, *op. cit.*, VIII, 54.

[8] Reilly, *The Visitation of Religious*, p. 50.

[9] C. un., *de statu regularium*, III, 16, in VI°.

[10] C. 2, *de statu monachorum vel canonicorum regularium*, III, 10, in Clem.

[11] Schroeder, *Disciplinary Decrees*, p. 453.

and the jurisdiction of the local ordinary through the acquisition of special privileges.[12]

The climax was reached at the V Lateran Council (1512–1517) when in a review of the entire question of exemptions the bishops were able to regain some of the authority they had lost. In the eleventh session, on December 19, 1516, Leo X (1513–1521) published the Bull *Dum intra mentis arcana,*[13] in which the bishops were given permission to "conduct a visitation of the parochial churches in charge of the regulars located within their territorial jurisdiction in all matters that pertained to the *cura animarum* and the administration of the Sacraments. Those found to be delinquent they were to punish, if religious, in accordance with the statutes of their order within the conventual enclosure." [14]

---

[12] Reilly, *The Visitation of Religious,* p. 51.

[13] Mansi, XXXII, 970–976; *Bullarum Diplomatum et Privilegiorum Sanctorum Romanorum Pontificum Taurinensis Editio* (25 vols., Augustae Taurinorum, 1857–1872), V, 685–687 (hereafter cited *Bull. Rom. Taur.*); Schroeder, *Disciplinary Decrees,* p. 506.

[14] Schroeder, *Disciplinary Decrees,* p. 506.

SECTION II

LEGISLATION FROM THE COUNCIL OF TRENT TO THE CODE (1918)

CHAPTER IV

RIGHTS OF THE BISHOP IN RELATION TO THE FOUNDATION OF CONGREGATIONS OF SIMPLE VOWS

Article 1. Early Religious Congregations

Innocent III (1198–1216) in the IV Lateran Council (1215) had emphatically decreed that no new orders were to be founded.[1] This in effect placed the approval of any new order exclusively in the hands of the Holy See, thus setting aside the legislation of the Council of Chalcedon (451), which had placed such power in the hands of the local ordinary.[2] This legislation of Innocent III had not been retracted up to the time of the Council of Trent, nor did that Council in any way subtract from or change this legislation. As far, then, as the written law was concerned, bishops did not possess this right of founding new institutes or of approving such institutes. Any violation of this law resulted not only in an illicit, but also in an invalid act.[3]

This presents a difficulty, for in point of fact bishops did, without the approval of the Holy See, found institutes within their dioceses. The proper explanation regarding this procedure seems to be that given by Bouix (1808–1870).[4] He held that a contrary custom was set up against the requirement of pontifical approval for new institutes through the repeated acts of the bishops with the tacit approval of the Holy See.

Prior, however, to any treatment of the existence of such a contrary custom, the discussion of a more fundamental problem claims attention in the light of the papal constitutions of the late

---

[1] C. 1, X, *de religiosis domibus*, III, 36.

[2] Mansi, VII, 359.

[3] Cf. the 23rd canon of the II Council of Lyons (1274), in which Gregory X (1271–1276) had abolished all orders that had come into existence subsequent to Pope Innocent's prohibition.—Mansi, XXIV, 96.

[4] Bouix, *De Jure Regularium*, I, 210.

sixteenth century, namely, the very right to existence for religious congregations whose members professed simple vows. While the Council of Trent did not legislate against new foundations, it did repeat the legislation of Boniface VIII on the question of the enclosure for nuns.[5] Pope Pius V (1566–1572) in his effort to enforce the observance of the cloister widened the scope of the Council's legislation to include not only nuns but all women religious. He accomplished this in his Constitution *Circa pastoralis,* issued on May 19, 1566,[6] by dissolving all congregations of women in that he required that they take solemn vows and observe the cloister. The Constitutions made specific mention simply of Tertiary groups, but in implied fact it thus forbade all simple vow congregations of women religious.[7]

Pius V followed up this Constitution with another on October 14, 1568, which forbade ordination for any religious not in solemn vows. The Jesuits had had the practice of requiring a period of probation for their religious before these were permitted to take solemn vows. During this period these religious had simple vows.[8] The Jesuits had indeed obtained the necessary permission to continue the probationary period with simple vows, but the legislation of the Constitution *Romanus Pontifex* in 1568 indicated the mind of Pius V and the general rule enacted by him with regard to religious congregations of men with simple vows.[9]

[5] Sess. XXV, *de regularibus,* c. 5.

[6] Const. *Circa pastoralis,* 29 maii 1566—*Codicis Iuris Canonici Fontes* (cura Emi Petri Card. Gasparri editi, 9 vols., Romae [later Civitate Vaticana]: Typis Polyglottis Vaticanis, 1923–1938. [Vols. VII–IX *ed. cura et studio Emi* Iustiniani Card. Serédi.]), n. 112 (hereafter cited *Fontes*).

[7] Bouix, *De Jure Regularium,* I, 219; Larraona, "Commentarium Codicis"—*Commentarium pro Religiosis* (Romae, 1920–1934; ab anno 1935: *Commentarium pro Religiosis et Missionariis*), I (1920), 47 (hereafter cited *CpR* and *CpRM* respectively); Vermeersch, *De Religiosis Institutis et Personis* (2 vols., Tom. I, 2. ed., 1907; Tom. II, 4. ed., 1909; *Supplementa et Monumenta,* 4. ed., Bruges, 1909), I, n. 3, p. 49 (hereafter cited *De Religiosis* and *Supplementa* respectively); Lucidi, *De Visitatione Sacrorum Liminum* (3. ed., 3 vols., ed. J. Schneider, Romae, 1883), II, 238.

[8] Const. "*Romanus Pontifex,*" 14 Oct. 1568—*Fontes,* n. 230.

[9] Cf. const., *Quam Fructuosius,* 1 febr. 1583—*Fontes,* n. 150. This constitution gave the Jesuits permission to profess their members with simple vows.

It was less than a month later that the Constitution *Lubricum vitae genus* was promulgated. In it there was a condemnation of all religious congregations of men who took only simple vows.[10] This condemnation included all such groups which lived in common, and wore a distinctive garb. The members of these groups accordingly had to take solemn vows.[11]

As will be seen later, these provisions of law were more honored in the breach rather than in the observance, and while the Holy See did attempt once again to enforce the above mentioned regulations, its policy became, especially with regard to the religious congregations of women, one of toleration. Its final approval of them came only in the nineteenth century.[12] It is a fact that as early as 1616—fifty years after the Constitution *Circa pastoralis*—there did exist congregations of women who professed simple vows and lived outside the cloister. Despite a decree of the Sacred Congregation of Bishops and Regulars (December 20, 1616) against them, they continued to exist.[13] Even at an earlier time Pius V never realized his desire of completely abolishing the congregations in which the members took only simple vows, or of enforcing the strict cloister for all religious.[14]

If this can be said of the religious congregations of women, it was even more manifest with reference to the religious congregations of men, for in the years following Pius' condemnation, there were repeated cases in which such institutes came into existence, and some even with the approval of the Holy See.[15]

---

[10] Const. "*Lubricum vitae genus*," 17 nov. 1568—*Bull. Rom. Taur.*, VII, 725.

[11] *Collectanea in Usum Secretariae Sacrae Congregationis Episcoporum et Regularium* (cura A. Bizzarri Archiepiscopi Phillipensis Secretarii edita, Romae: Ex Typographia Polyglotta, S. C. de Propaganda Fide, 1885), p. 743, footnote (hereafter cited *Collectanea*).

[12] Larraona, "Commentarium Codicis"—*CpR*, I (1920), 46.

[13] Bulla, *Pretiosus*, 25 maii 1727—*Bull. Rom. Taur.*, XXII, 522–542.

[14] Lucidi, *De Visitatione Sacrorum Liminum*, II, n. 264; Bouix, *De Jure Regularium*, I, 326.

[15] Thus there were such institutes as the following: the Oratorians of St. Philip Neri, approved by Gregory XIII, const. *Copiosus*, 15 iul. 1575—*Bull. Rom. Taur.*, VIII, 541; Clerics Regular of the Mother of God, approved by Clement VIII (1592–1605), const. *Ex quo divina*, 3 oct. 1595—*Bull. Rom.*

In further proof of the attitude of benign toleration on the part of the Holy See during the latter seventeenth and early eighteenth centuries, one may point to two papal constitutions. In the Constitution *Alias propositas* Clement IX (1667–1669) granted certain favors to a group of women who lived in common with the profession of simple vows.[16] And in 1727, Benedict XIII (1724–1730) expressly stated that he did not wish to prohibit the existence of tertiaries who took simple vows. In his Constitution this pope pointed out the fact that such groups had been in existence as early as the year 1616.[17]

But the policy of tolerance had by no means become entrenched, for in 1737 Clement XII (1730–1740) revoked the Bull of Benedict XIII, as well as all the favors and privileges which had been given with it. The situation once more became similar to that which had prevailed after Pius V's condemnation.[18] But the pronouncement of Clement XII marked the last of that nature to issue from the Holy See.

It remained for Benedict XIV (1740–1758), a gifted and learned canonist, to give some rights and privileges in the eyes of the law to these groups. This he did in his famous Constitution *Quamvis iusto*. In this Constitution, without giving approval to the institute of simple vows itself, Benedict approved the rules of the Congregation of the English Ladies, but did not accord them the rank of true religious, since they professed only simple vows. Thus the way was opened for a legitimate and juridical existence on the part of congregations whose members made profession of simple vows only.[19]

After the presentation of these historical points as affecting the

---

Taur., X, 411; the Poor Clerics of the Mother of God of Pious Schools, approved by Paul V (1605–1621), const. *Ad ea*, 6 mart. 1617—*Bull. Rom. Taur.*, XII, 382.

[16] Const., *Alias propositas*, 10 dec. 1667—*Bull. Rom. Taur.*, XVII, 609, 610.

[17] Bulla *Pretiosus*, 25 maii 1727—*Bull. Rom. Taur.*, XXII, 522–542.

[18] Const., *Romanus Pontifex*, 30 mart. 1737—*Bull. Rom. Taur.*, XXIII, 323–327.

[19] Const. *Quamvis iusto*, 30 par. 1749—*Fontes*, n. 398; Larraona, "Commentarium Codicis"—*CpR*, I (1920), 49; Schäfer, *De Religiosis*, n. 13.

legitimate and juridical existence of religious congregations, it is now appropriate to consider the existence, through a long and sustained custom, of the right of the local ordinary to erect such congregations independently of the approval of the Holy See. As early as February 14, 1501, Alexander VI (1492–1503) in the Bull *Ea quae* gave approval to an institute which had been founded some years earlier with the sole permission of the local ordinary. This was the group founded by St. Jeanne of Valois.[20] So also the Society of Mary (members called Marists) was founded originally with only the approval of the local bishop, though later it did receive papal approval through the Bull *Omnium gentium* of Gregory XVI (1831–1846) under date of April 29, 1836.[21]

There are many other instances, especially in France, of congregations of women established with the authority of the bishop alone. It must be concluded from this that the law requiring pontifical permission for the founding of religious institutes either did not embrace institutes whose members took only simple vows, or through the force of contrary custom had fallen into disuse. Some writers argue that since congregations whose members took only simple vows were not in existence at the time when the IV General Council of the Lateran (1215) legislated against the founding of new institutes,[22] it can be assumed that the legislator had no intention of prohibiting them or their foundation.[23] But, since Innocent III's prohibition extended to all existing orders, and since it employed the general term "*religio*," the law seems

---

[20] Heimbucher, *Die Orden und Kongregationen der katholischen Kirche* (3. ed., 2 vols., Paderborn, 1933–1934), I, 627–628.

[21] Bulla *Omnium gentium,* 29 apr. 1836—*Acta Gregorii Papae XVI* (4 vols., Romae, Ex Typographia Polyglotta S. C. de Propaganda Fide, 1901–1904), II, 107.

[22] C. 1, X, *de religiosis domibus,* III, 36.

[23] Vicente, *Recentia Instituta* (Madrid, 1916), n. 58; Toso, *Ad Codicem Iuris Canonici Commentaria Minora* (5 vols., Romae: Marietti, 1920–1927), lib. II, pars II, p. 14 (hereafter cited *Commentaria Minora;* Chelodi, *Ius de Personis iuxta Codicem Iuris Canonici, Praemisso Tractatu de Principiis et Fontibus Iuris Canonici* (ed. altera, a Sac. Ernesto Bertagnolli recognita et aucta, Tridenti: Libr. Edit. Tridentum, 1927), p. 411; footnote n. 1 (hereafter cited *Ius de Personis*).

to have extended also to such congregations. The derogating force of custom in relation to the written law seems to offer a better explanation of the existence of the bishop's right to approve congregations in which simple vows alone were taken.[24]

Article 2. The Nineteenth Century

It is difficult to say just when this custom obtained the force of law. The fact of the Holy See's acknowledgment of the legal force of this custom is a matter which stands plainly revealed in the nineteenth century.

It was the French Revolution with its drastic consequences for the monasteries and orders with solemn vows that accorded the occasion for the changed attitude of the Holy See towards simple vow congregations. As a result of laws passed during the French Revolution, monasteries lost the recognition of their moral personality, and with it their ability to hold property.[25] The Holy See had to suspend the effects of solemn vows.[26] This, combined with the far-reaching good that the members of simple vow institutes were able to accomplish as teachers, as nurses and as guardians of the poor and the aged, led the Holy See to extend a more gracious attitude towards such institutes.[27] No longer did the Holy See give only a very limited approval to such institutes; rather, it accorded a complete approval with no reservations.

As early as 1821 a Congregation of Women obtained papal approval both for its constitutions and for the institute itself.[28] The

---

[24] Bouix, *De Jure Regularium,* I, 212. It is to be noted that the greater weight of authority holds that congregations were bound by this prohibition of Innocent III. Cf. Bizzarri, *Collectanea,* p. 742; Bouix, *De Jure Regularium,* I, 201; Wernz, *Ius Decretalium,* III, n. 608; Suarez, *Opera Omnia,* III, L. II, c. 16, n. 18; Pejška, *Ius Canonicum Religiosorum* (3. ed., Friburgi in Brisgovia: Herder, 1927), p. 13.

[25] Larraona, "Commentarium Codicis"—*CpR,* I (1920), 133.

[26] Bizzarri, *Collectanea,* pp. 72, 86, 412, 451, 454.

[27] Bouix, *De Jure Regularium,* I, 388. Bouix noted the fact that the civil law in France recognized only simple vows, and these for a period of five years at most.

[28] Bizzarri, "Annotationes"—*Archiv für katholisches Kirchenrecht* (Innsbruck, 1857–1861; Mainz, 1862–) XV, (1866), 441. This was the Congregation of the Sacred Heart of Mary, so approved on Sept. 14, 1821.

words "*citra tamen approbationem conservatorii,*" which up to that time had accompanied all such papal approvals, were omitted entirely.[29] It is important to note, however, that papal approval was not forthcoming until the particular institute had been established for some time and had given evidence of its strength and ability to endure. Until such a time was reached, it was the local ordinary who gave the initial approval and under whose guidance the congregation developed.[30] This certainly was at least an implicit recognition of the right of the bishop to found such groups.

As the petitions for papal approbation grew more numerous, a method was adopted by the Sacred Congregation of Bishops and Regulars to be used as a norm in the approving of institutes of simple vows.[31] Whenever a petition was received by the Sacred Congregation, accompanied with letters of commendation from the bishops of the places where the institute had houses, the request was forwarded to the bishop of that diocese in which the first foundation had taken place or where the motherhouse was located. He was to report on the end or scope of the institute, the number of houses, the number of members, its means of support, the progress it had made, and all such points.[32]

The extent of papal approbation varied according to the particular institute's variable status of stability. Thus, if an institute was only recently founded and possessed only one or the other house, it would receive praise for its end or scope, while another institute might receive an approval for itself, but not for its constitutions. The constitutions were not approved until their worth was established upon a proper period of probation, and only after all the necessary changes had been made.[33] The action of the Sacred Congregation in granting these decrees of praise for the more fully developed institutes was a forerunner of the sub-

---

[29] Schäfer, *De Religiosis,* n. 13.

[30] Bizzarri, *Collectanea,* p. 772.

[31] Bizzarri, *Collectanea,* pp. 772–773.

[32] Bizzarri, *loc. cit.;* Lucidi, *De Visitatione Sacrorum Liminum,* II, p. 256, n. 283.

[33] Bizzarri, *Collectanea,* p. 773.

sequent action of Leo XIII (1878–1903) in classifying institutes into those of pontifical and those of diocesan approval.[34]

With the Holy See's attitude as changed from the practice of a mere act of toleration to an act of praise and encouragement, simple vow congregations increased rapidly during the nineteenth century. In the period from 1814 to 1862 alone, one hundred and twenty-four of these congregations sought papal approval.[35] It was this rapid increase in numbers that caused Pope Pius IX (1846–1878) to issue to the bishops of the world a letter in which he expressed concern over the perhaps needless multiplication of such institutes. The occasion for invoking a restraining action was presented to the Vatican Council, but the Council ended too suddenly to permit any such action to be taken on the matter.[36] Two recorded responses as received from bishops of France and of Belgium both favored the new Congregations, and one response, likewise received from France, even urged their increase.[37]

To be noted here is the fact that various particular councils of France and of Germany felt a definite need to express in law the requirement of episcopal consent for the erection of any religious congregation.[38] The reason given for the enactment of such legislation was either that of preventing further violations or of clarifying the unwritten universal law.[39] The Plenary Council of Latin America (1899) similarly restated the right of bishops, to

---

[34] Const. *Conditae a Christo,* 8 dec. 1900—*Fontes,* n. 644.

[35] Bizzarri, *Collectanea,* p. 808.

[36] Pius IX wrote on June 6, 1867: "Plures prodierunt et in dies prodeunt Congregationes et Instituta virorum et mulierum, qui votis simplicibus obstricti, piis muneribus obeundis se addicunt. Expeditne ut potius Congregationes ab Apostolica Sede probatae augeantur latius et crescant, quam ut novae eundem finem habentes constituantur et efformentur."—Cf. *Acta et Decreta Sacrorum Conciliorum Recentiorum, Collectio Lacensis* (7 vols., Friburgi Brisgoviae, 1870–1890), VII, 1028 (hereafter cited *Coll. Lac.*).

[37] *Coll. Lac.,* VII, 837a; VII, 877a.

[38] Cf. The Provincial Council of Tours (1849)—*Coll. Lac.,* IV, 278d; The Provincial Council of Rheims (1849)—*Coll. Lac.,* IV, 144; The Provincial Council of Rouen (1850)—*Coll. Lac.,* IV, 532d; The Provincial Council of Bordeaux (1850)—*Coll. Lac.,* IV, 603; The Provincial Council of Prague (1860)—*Coll. Lac.,* V, 572b; The Provincial Council of Utrecht (1865)—*Coll. Lac.,* V, 896–897.

[39] Orth, *The Approbation of Religious Institutes,* p. 68.

the exclusion of their subordinates, to found and erect religious institutes.[40]

In the East, the Oriental Church was already separated from Rome at the time of the IV Lateran Council (1215). When it united again with Rome (1439), the Oriental Church was not bound by the legislation of the IV Lateran Council, among the provisions of which was one which had reserved exclusively to the Holy See the right of approval for new religious orders. The Oriental Church retained the legislation of the Council of Chalcedon (451), which had given to the ordinary of the place the right to found new monasteries.[41]

Article 3. Legislation immediately Preceding the Code

The Constitution *Conditae a Christo* of Pope Leo XIII (Dec. 8, 1900), called the *Magna Charta* of simple vow congregations, gave to these institutes a juridical character and standing within the frame work of the written laws of the Church.[42] It established two types of simple vow congregations: the diocesan institute (those with only episcopal approbation) and the pontifical institute (those which had obtained papal approval either for the institute itself or for its constitutions).[43] With this distinction made, the Constitution treated each type separately, and first the diocesan institutes. The bishop's right to approve congregations was formally recognized, but at the same time limited through the demand that certain requirements be met before an institute could receive approval.

First the bishops were to ascertain whether the institute in question contained in its constitutions anything against faith and morals, or anything against the sacred canons and the decrees of the Pontiffs, and whether the regulations in the Constitutions were

---

[40] *Acta et Decreta Concilii Plenarii Americae Latinae in Urbe Celebrati anno 1899* (Romae, 1902), n. 322.

[41] Cf. Synod of Mount Lebanon: " Non possunt nova erigi monasteria sine consensu Ordinarii loci, ut sacra praecipit Chalcedonensis Synodus."—*Coll. Lac.*, II, 355.

[42] Larraona, " Commentarium Codicis "—*CpR,* I (1920), 171, n. 17.

[43] *Acta Sanctae Sedis* (41 vols., Romae, 1865–1908), XXXIII (1900), 341 (hereafter cited *ASS*).

suited for the attainment of the end of the institute.[44] No new institutes were to be established without episcopal approval, and this was not to be given until the prospective founders who sought the bishop's approval had been duly examined on the probity of their lives, and on the prudence of their motives in their desire to found an institute.[45] Finally, if there already existed institutes which professed and prosecuted the same end or purpose, then the bishops were to welcome such institutes into the diocese rather than to establish new ones.[46]

In the following year (1901) appeared a set of instructions issued to bishops by the Sacred Congregation of Bishops and Regulars. These instructions outlined the requisite procedure in the obtaining of pontifical approval.[47] However, these *Normae* had no force of law, and were later supplanted by the *Normae* of 1921.[48]

Following the issuance of the Constitution *Conditae a Christo,* a great many diocesan congregations came into existence, some of which did not warrant approval in the mind of the Holy See. To remedy such a situation through the exercise of a greater degree of prudence on the part of bishops in granting permission for the erection of new institutes, Pius X in a Motu proprio (*Dei providentis*) set up new requirements that were to be met before an institute was to receive episcopal approval. Chief among these was the one that demanded consultation with the Holy See before the granting of the approval.[49]

In the letter which requested this approval, the bishop had to give detailed information on the name and character of the founder of the institute, on the reason for the foundation, on the name or title of the institute, on the form and color of the habit to be

---

[44] Const. *Conditae a Christo,* § I, n. i—*Fontes,* n. 644.

[45] Const. *Conditae a Christo,* § 1, n. 2—*Fontes,* n. 644.

[46] Const. *Conditae a Christo,* § I, n. 3—*Fontes,* n. 644.

[47] *Normae secundum quas S. Cong. Episcoporum et Regularium procedere solet in approbandis Novis Institutes Votorum Simplicium* (Romae: Typis S. Cong. de Propaganda Fide, 1901).

[48] *Acta Apostolicae Sedis, Commentarium Officiale* (Romae, 1909–), XIII (1921), 312–319) (hereafter cited *AAS*).

[49] Pius X, Motu proprio *Dei providentis,* 16 iul. 1906—*Fontes,* n. 675.

worn by the novices and the professed, on the purpose of the institute, on its means of support, and finally on whether or not there were other institutes in the diocese which prosecuted similar work.[50]

Once the institute had been duly established, no changes could be made in the above listed matters without the approval of the Holy See.[51] Through this Motu proprio of Pius X, the controlling decision as to the need and fitness of any new institute was solely the Holy See's to make, and thus there was enacted in substance the legislation which is now contained in the Code.[52]

---

[50] *Ibid.*, § I: "Nullus episcopus aut cuiusvis loci Ordinarius, nisi habita Apostolica Sedis per litteras licentia, novam alterutrius sexus sodalitatem condat aut in sua dioecesi condi permittat."—*Fontes*, n. 675. *Ibid.*, § II: "Ordinarius, huius licentiae impetrandae gratia, Sacrum Consilium Episcoporum et Regularium negotiis praepositum adeat per libellum supplicem, quo haec docebit: quis qualisque sit novae sodalitatis auctor, et qua is causa ad eam institutendam ducatur; quibus verbis conceptum sit sodalitatis condendae nomen seu titulus; quae sit forma, color, materia, partes habitus a novitiis et professis gestandi; quot et quaenam sibi opera sodalitas assumptura sit; quibus opibus tuitio eiusdem contineatur; an similia in dioecesi sint instituta, et quibus illa operibus insistant."—*Fontes*, n. 675.

[51] *Ibid.*, § III—*Fontes*, n. 675.

[52] Canon 492, § 1.

CHAPTER V

RIGHTS OF THE BISHOP IN RELATION TO VISITATION

ARTICLE 1. THE COUNCIL OF TRENT (1545–1563)

The bishop as the ordinary and immediate pastor of the faithful in his diocese has as one of his rights and duties the visitation of his diocese that he may the better preserve sound doctrine, safeguard good morals, correct evils, and promote peace, piety and discipline.[1] This legislation has its counterpart in the legislation of the Council of Trent, which made such a great effort to reform abuses in the Church. Thus the bishops were given the right and authority, even as delegates of the Holy See, to decree, to regulate, and even under threat of penalty to execute those things which in their prudence should appear to them as necessary for the correction of their subjects and the promotion of the good of their dioceses.[2] And while the privileges of exemption still remained in force according to the extent in which it had been granted in each particular case, the Council of Trent did define more accurately the bishops' powers of visitation, especially over nuns subject to them or directly subject to the Holy See, as well as over the churches which had the care of souls with relation to secular persons.

Thus the Council, in renewing the Constitution *Periculoso* of Boniface VIII (1294–1303),[3] commanded all bishops to make it their special care that in all monasteries of nuns subject to them by their own authority, or by the authority of the Holy See, any violations of the cloister should be corrected, and if no violations had taken place, that they might be prevented. The bishops were

[1] Can. 343, § 1.

[2] *Canones et Decreta Sacrosancti Oecumenici Concilii Tridentini* (Romae, 1904), sess. XXIV, *de ref.*, c. 10.

[3] C. un., *de statu regularium,* III, 16, in VIº.

to take whatever means were necessary even to the point of employing ecclesiastical penalties and of calling for aid from the secular arm, in their effort to safeguard the observance of the enclosure.[4] All monasteries of nuns directly subject to the Holy See were to be supervised by the bishops in their capacity of delegates of the Holy See.[5]

In the matter of churches subject to the care of monasteries, the Council decreed that, in monasteries of men or of women to which there was attached the care of souls for secular persons who did not belong to the household of the monastery, the persons exercising the care of souls were in all things that pertained to it, as well as in the administration of the sacraments, subject to the jurisdiction, visitation and correction of the bishop in whose diocese they were located. Appointments were to be made only after the consent of the bishop had been duly obtained, and after the candidate had been examined by the bishop or his vicar. An exception to this requirement obtained for the Abbey of Cluny and its territories, for those monasteries or places in which abbots, generals or heads of orders had their principal residence, and for other monasteries and houses in which abbots or other superiors of regulars exercised episcopal and temporal jurisdiction over the parish priests and parishioners.[6]

Benefices which were held by monasteries, if such benefices had the care of souls attached, were to be visited yearly by the local ordinary for the sake of insuring the proper fulfillment of that responsibility through competent vicars; appeals, privileges and exemptions were to no avail in the aforesaid matter.[7]

The Council further ordered that local ordinaries were bound to visit every year with apostolic authority all churches in whatever manner exempt, and to provide with proper remedies of law that those churches that needed repair be repaired, and that they be not in any way defrauded of the care of souls, if annexed to them, or of other services due them.[8]

---

[4] Sess. XXV, *de regularibus*, c. 5.
[5] Sess. XXV, *de regularibus*, c. 9.
[6] Sess. XXV, *de regularibus*, c. 11.
[7] Sess. VII, *de ref.*, c. 7.
[8] Sess. VII, *de ref.*, c. 8.

Article 2. Early Religious Congregations

As has been noted in the preceding chapter, Pius V (1566–1572), in his effort to enforce the Tridentine legislation on the observance of the cloister for nuns, dissolved all congregations of women with simple vows.[9] In a later Constitution[10] he abolished all simple vow congregations of men. History bears out the fact, however, that his successors did give approval to congregations of men, even to the point of granting to some of them certain exemptions from episcopal visitation, and of granting as well a certain kind of juridical existence to congregations of women under the jurisdiction and visitation of the local ordinary.[11]

Alexander VII (1655–1667) gave to the Congregation of the Missions, founded in 1625, exemption from the jurisdiction of the bishop in all things, except with relation to those members of the Congregation who were appointed to missions under the bishop, to whom, however, they were made subject only in those matters which pertained to the missions themselves.[12]

When Benedict XIV (1740–1758) in his Constitution *Quamvis iusto* gave approval to the English Ladies, an institute of simple vows, he also defined their relationship with the local ordinary. They were to be subject to the local ordinary in whose diocese they were located, and it was the local ordinary who was to appoint their confessors and spiritual directors.[13]

The office of superioress general was indeed permitted to exist, but it was so limited and restricted in its powers that it might not in any way lessen the jurisdiction of the local ordinary. The superioress general was allowed with the bishop's permission to visit the community's houses situated in his diocese, in order to ascertain the manner in which discipline was observed, and in order to supervise the educational activities of the sisters. She was required, however, to submit a report on this to the local

---

[9] Const. *Circa pastoralis,* 29 maii 1566—*Fontes,* n. 112.

[10] Const. *Lubricum vitae genus,* 17 nov. 1568—*Bull. Rom. Taur.,* VII, 725.

[11] Benedictus XIV, *Institutiones Ecclesiasticae* (Prati, 1844), XXIX, n. 13.

[12] Const. *Ex commissa,* 22 sept. 1655—*Bull. Rom. Taur.,* XVII, p. 68.

[13] Const. *Quamvis iusto,* 30 apr. 1749, § 13—*Fontes,* n. 398.

ordinary, who was to avail himself of this report in the direction of the institute.[14]

The Congregation of the Discalced Passionists in 1769 obtained the privilege of exemption from episcopal visitation as far as the houses of the institute were concerned.[15] The Redemptorists received this privilege of exemption in 1789, and the Congregation of Pious Workers in 1792.[16]

In the above-mentioned cases explicit grants of exemption were given to individual congregations, but in a famous decision rendered by Benedict XIV (1740–1758)[17] the relationship between a local ordinary and a pontifically approved non-exempt congregation was determined to some degree. The Congregation of the Oratory of St. Philip Neri had asked a series of questions of the Holy See concerning the rights and duties of a certain archbishop in whose diocese they were established. Pope Benedict XIV decreed that the local ordinary in his visitation had no right to inspect the books required by the constitutions of the congregation. The only books he could investigate were those which contained the inventory of the vestments of the church. The local ordinary had no authority over the bursar of the congregation in reference to expenses and financial reports.

How far the provisions of this decision were applicable to other similar institutes is not entirely clear. Bouix maintained that, since the Oratorians were not an exempt congregation, the points decided in this reply could be applied to other similar groups of non-exempt congregations approved by the Holy See, whether they professed simple vows or none at all.[18] Others seemed to demand an explicit exemption from the local ordinary's power through a grant of privilege from the Holy See, so that in the

---

[14] Const. *Quamvis iusto,* 30 apr. 1749—*Fontes,* n. 398.

[15] Const. *Supremi apostolatus,* 16 dec., 1769—*Bullarii Romani Continuatio Summorum Pontificum* (14 vols., Prati, 1843–1867), VII, 73 (hereafter cited *Bull. Rom. Con.*).

[16] For the Redemptorists, cf. Const. *Sacrosanctum apostolatus,* 21 aug. 1789—*Bull. Rom. Con.,* X, 2111; for the Congregation of Pious Workers, cf. const. *Inter multiplices,* 14 dec. 1792—*Bull. Rom. Con.,* X, 2569.

[17] Bulla *Emanavit,* 21 ian. 1758—Bizzarri, *Collectanea,* 434–435.

[18] Bouix, *De Jure Regularium,* II, 379.

case of most of the religious congregations of men and women there remained the right and the duty of the local ordinary to visit the churches, the houses, and the members of these institutes.[19] But this right never extended to the rules and constitutions of the institutes approved by Rome, as is evident from the responses given by the Holy See.[20] It seems entirely proper to infer from this that those congregations which existed with the sole approval of the bishop were completely subject to him in the matter of visitation.

The point of view which held for the subjection of such congregations to the visitation of the bishop seems to be sustained by a decision given by the Sacred Congregation of Bishops and Regulars concerning the Oblates of the Blessed Virgin Mary and their exemption from the local ordinaries. In a petition sent to the Sacred Congregation, the Oblates sought to ascertain whether or not they were subject to the local ordinary and, if so, in what manner. In an answer given on July 28, 1837, the Sacred Congregation maintained that they were subject to the visitation of the bishop. Since however there was involved the interpretation of privileges already acquired,[21] the entire matter was referred to the Holy Father, Gregory XVI (1831–1846), who, in resolving the doubt, subjected the congregation to the visitation of the bishop as regards their churches alone, but not in the matter of the internal discipline and administration of the congregation.[22] In his reply, Pope Gregory XVI indicated that the decision as given resulted in virtue of a previous grant of exemption in which the congregation participated. In the light of this reply any congregation not similarly exempted still was subject to the visitation of the bishop even with regard to the internal discipline of the congregation.

---

[19] Schmalzgrueber, *Ius Ecclesiasticum Universum,* Lib. III, Titulus XXXVI, n. 4; Lucidi, *De Visitatione Sacrorum Liminum* III, nn. 436, 437.

[20] Bizzarri, *Collectanea,* p. 434; S. C. Ep. et Reg., 27 febr., 1863—*Fontes,* n. 1987.

[21] *Analecta Juris Pontificii* (Romae, 1855–1869; Parisiis, 1872–1891), XII (1870), col. 1019, n. 863.

[22] Vermeersch, *Supplementa,* pp. 400–401.

ARTICLE 3. LEGISLATION IMMEDIATELY PRECEDING THE CODE

All doubt, however, about the extent of the bishop's power of visitation was ended with the Constitution *Conditae a Christo,* issued by Leo XIII (1878–1903) on December 8, 1900.[23] In reference to institutes of diocesan approval this Constitution decreed that the bishop had the right to visit any house in his diocese in matters which concerned the attainment of virtue, the maintenance of discipline and the administration of temporal goods.[24]

In regard to institutes of pontifical approval there was some restriction on his right of visitation. He could visit the church, the sacristy, the public oratory, the place for confessions, and in so doing provide for whatever necessary corrections were needed. In clerical institutes of pontifical approval the bishop could exercise no right of visitation in matters of discipline, of conscience, or with reference to the administration of temporal goods. In lay institutes of men and women of pontifical approval, however, the bishop retained his right of visitation in matters affecting discipline, doctrine and morals, the enclosure and the frequentation of the sacraments. In the matter of their temporal goods his right was limited to an examination of the administration of funds received for divine worship or for the benefit of the locality or diocese.

In all these matters as affecting congregations of pontifical approval, the bishop had to refer the making of corrections to the general of the institute. The bishop himself could act immediately in two situations—first, if the matter itself was such as to demand immediate action, and secondly, if after referring the matter to the general, the latter failed to act.[25]

These were the general laws which, as enacted in the Constitution, governed the visitation of such institutes of diocesan and pontifical approval. But the Constitution expressly took into account any privileges or faculties granted to these institutes in particular cases by the Holy See, as well as those which had

---

[23] Const. *Conditae a Christo—Fontes,* n. 644.

[24] Const. *Conditae a Christo,* § I, n. X—*Fontes,* n. 644.

[25] *Ibid.,* § II, n. XI—*Fontes,* n. 644.

become established through immemorial custom. Exception was also made for any particular legislation contained in the constitutions of any institute approved by the Holy See.[26]

There was no further legislation on the rights and duties of the local ordinary in reference to the visitation of congregations until the promulgation of the Code. There was, however, a clarification of the nature of institutes of diocesan approval through the Constitution *Dei providentis* of Pius X (1903–1914), in which the pope made it clear that even though an institute of diocesan approval was established in several dioceses, it was still diocesan in nature, until it received the decree of praise from the Holy See.[27] And thus such an institute was still subject to the visitation of the ordinary of each diocese in which it had a foundation, as had been indicated according to the rules enacted in the Constitution *Conditae a Christo*.

---

[26] *Ibid.*, § II, n. XII—*Fontes*, n. 644.

[27] Pius X, const. *Dei providentis*, 16 iul. 1906—*Fontes*, n. 675.

CHAPTER VI

RIGHTS OF THE BISHOP IN RELATION TO ELECTIONS

ARTICLE 1. THE COUNCIL OF TRENT

In the election of abbots, superiors and other officials of orders and monasteries, no provision was made in the Tridentine law for the presence of the local ordinary. As will be pointed out, this was to remain true also with relation to the religious congregations of men in the election of their superiors. The Council of Trent did, however, grant to the local ordinary the right to preside at the election of the abbess, the prioress, and the superioress.[1]

In the event that no one was to be found in the monastery who possessed the necessary qualifications for the position, the bishop was given the right to permit them to elect someone from another monastery. If he considered this inadvisable, he could grant them permission to elect one of the members of their monastery who had been previously disqualified because of age.[2] The bishop did not possess the right to enter the enclosure for the election, but was required to receive the vote at the grating. This was the extent of the Council of Trent's rule on the rights and duties of the local ordinary in the election of the abbess or the superioress of a monastery of nuns.

ARTICLE 2. EARLY RELIGIOUS CONGREGATIONS

It is the famous Constitution *Quamvis iusto* of Benedict XIV (1740–1758) that offered the first indication of the rôle of the superioress general in religious congregations of women in relation to the ordinary of the diocese. Benedict XIV indicated in this Constitution that such an office was of value to the institute,

[1] Sess. XXV, *de regularibus et monialibus*, c. 7.

[2] Sess. XXV, *de regularibus et monialibus*, c. 7.

and he set down in paragraph twenty-two of the Constitution a method already in use in the election of a person for such a position.[3] Referring to two societies of women with simple vows, originally founded in Rome and since spread to other dioceses, Benedict noted that the election of the superioress general took place in the presence of the spiritual director appointed by the local ordinary. The consultors for the congregation were also elected in the presence of the spiritual director.

Once elected, the superioress general was to serve without infringing upon the jurisdiction of the local ordinary to whom the congregation was immediately subject. The right of the bishop to preside either personally or through a delegate at these elections in the congregations of women was to remain his through the following centuries down to the present time. It remains substantially the same in the Code, with only slight modifications.[4]

A response from the Sacred Congregation for Bishops and Regulars given on January 21, 1758, decided that congregations of men, if the members professed simple vows, but the institute was approved by the Holy See, were in no way subject to the local ordinary in the matter of the election of their superiors and of other officials of the congregations.[5] This reply was given in favor of the Oratorians. But inasmuch as the Oratorians were a non-exempt institute, this same rule was held to apply to other similar institutes of pontifical approval.[6] This same reply further decided that the bishop was the competent judge in any case arising out of a contention against the legitimate election of a superior, but he could act only when the case was brought before his tribunal by a member of the congregation.[7]

Bouix maintained, however, that the right to judge the legitimacy of an election pertained to the bishop only in that instance in which the election in question was that of a local superior, made by the religious of the congregation who were stationed in the diocese. The reply, according to this interpretation, did not con-

---

[3] Const. *Quamvis iusto,* 30 apr. 1749, § 22—*Fontes,* n. 398.

[4] Cf. can. 506, § 4; can. 508, § 4.

[5] Bizzarri, *Collectanea,* p. 434.

[6] Bouix, *De Jure Regularium,* II, 379.

[7] Bizzarri, *Collectanea,* p. 435.

template the election of a superior made by the general chapter of a congregation which had houses in many dioceses. To have such a power would have implied for the local ordinary a jurisdiction which extended beyond his diocese. In such cases the Holy See or its delegate alone was competent to make the decision.[8]

Article 3. The Nineteenth Century

In the nineteenth century the "*animadversiones*" of the Sacred Congregation for Bishops and Regulars give the best indication of the position of the bishop in this matter both as to actual practice as well as to the desire of the Holy See. The "*animadversiones*" were the observations on the constitutions of religious congregations when the constitutions were submitted to the Sacred Congregation for approval. These "*animadversiones*" were made with a view to correcting the constitutions to make them conform with the mind of the Holy See. Bizzarri published many of these "*animadversiones*" in his *Collectanea.* Among these various "*animadversiones*" were many which dealt with the rights and duties of the local ordinary in the matter of elections, and thus reflected a clear indication of what was not within his scope or power. Thus, in the religious congregations of men, bishops were not to be readily admitted as the presiding officer in chapters, and the newly elected superior general was to be confirmed in office with the exclusive permission of the Sacred Congregation of Bishops and Regulars.[9]

In reference to the religious congregations of women the following points were repeatedly made. The Apostolic See did not approve of bishops as superiors general of congregations which were spread into several dioceses, lest the jurisdiction of the individual bishops in their dioceses be in any way hampered.[10] Those constitutions which provided for the appointment of the superioress general by the bishop were to be changed in order that her election would be procured by a secret vote of the general chapter.[11]

[8] Bouix, *De Jure Regularium,* II, 380.

[9] Bizzarri, *Collectanea,* p. 790. These *animadversiones* covered the years 1858 to 1861.

[10] Bizzarri, *op. cit.,* pp. 792, 785.

[11] Bizzarri, *ibid.,* p. 788.

Through these responses of the Holy See it is possible to ascertain that prior to their approval by the Holy See certain religious congregations of women were subject to the bishops as their superiors general, while other congregations had their superioresses general appointed by the bishops apart from any consideration of the will of the general chapter of the congregations. The bishop who exercised these powers was the one in whose diocese the congregation had its origin or its mother house. The Holy See resisted all efforts of aggrandizement or control on the part of bishops in this matter, for it required the free and secret election of the superioress general in that it vindicated for the bishop the simple right to preside at the election as the delegate of the Holy See.[12]

Article 4. Legislation immediately Preceding the Code

No further change took place in the relationship between bishops and religious congregations in the matter of elections until the promulgation of the Constitution *Conditae a Christo* by Leo XIII (1878–1903) on December 8, 1900.[13] In this Constitution no mention was made of the bishop as possessing any right in the elections of the religious congregations of men professed with simple vows. In the congregations of women of diocesan approval, it was the bishop's right to preside either personally or through a delegate at the election of the superioress, and to confirm or veto the election according to the judgment of his conscience.[14]

In congregations of pontifical approval the bishop of the place where the election was held had the right to preside at the election as a delegate of the Holy See, but no mention was made of the power of the bishop to confirm or veto the election, as was the case in diocesan congregations.[15] The bishop could subdelegate this right of presiding at the elections in pontifically approved religious congregations of women. This right of presiding at the election of superioresses was later restricted by the Sacred Con-

---

[12] Maroto, "Annotationes," *CpR,* II (1921), 324.

[13] Const., *Conditae a Christo—Fontes,* n. 644.

[14] *Ibid.,* § I, n. IX—*Fontes,* n. 644.

[15] *Ibid.,* § II, n. 1—*Fontes,* n. 644.

gregation to the election of the superioress general alone,[16] and this limitation was confirmed by the Code.[17]

---

[16] Bastien, *Directoire Canonique a l'Usage des Congregations à Voeux Simples* (3. ed., Bruges: Beyaert, 1923), n. 303 (hereafter cited *Directoire Canonique*).

[17] Cf. canon 508, § 4.

CHAPTER VII

RIGHTS OF THE BISHOP IN RELATION TO THE ADMISSION OF CANDIDATES AND THE DISMISSAL OF RELIGIOUS

Article 1. The Council of Trent

No rights were given to the bishop regarding the admission of candidates to the various orders and monasteries of men, but the bishop was to receive a full report on any religious who wished to leave the monastery for any reason. The religious was to make this report, informing the bishop of the reasons for his desire to leave.[1] But the Council of Trent did legislate on the bishop's duty to examine carefully the candidates for orders, and also those who sought admission to the monasteries of women.

It was the bishop's task either personally, or through his vicar, or by means of a delegate to examine the desire of the aspirant, to ascertain her freedom in entering, to test her knowledge of what she was doing, to appraise her qualifications for the religious life, and to assay the suitableness of the monastery for that life. This examination was to be made before the reception of the habit, and again before the profession of vows.

The obligation rested upon the superioress to inform the bishop one month before the profession that the time was approaching for the profession of the first vows. For the non-fulfillment of this obligation the superioress was liable to suspension from office for as long a period as the bishop deemed proper. The Council set no definite time limit within which the bishop was to be notified that the time was approaching for the reception of the habit. He was, however, to be notified in due time, so that he could properly examine every candidate before her reception of the habit.[2]

[1] Sess. XXV, *de regularibus*, c. 19.

[2] Sess. XXV, *de regularibus*, c. 17.

Article 2. Early Religious Congregations

When Benedict XIV (1740–1758) accorded juridical existence to religious congregations of women in his Constitution *Quamvis iusto,* he furnished also in that same Constitution the rules governing the profession of the novices. The bishop alone could grant the necessary permission for the profession of vows, and the profession itself was to be made in his hands personally or through his delegate.[3] In the Constitution there was no explicit mention of the bishop's duty to examine the candidates, but in the light of the provisions of the Council of Trent, as also of the legislation that followed, this examination remained the duty of the bishop.

Regarding the religious congregations of men there seemed to be no provisions for the exercise of any supervision by the bishop in the matter of the acceptance of candidates. In 1837 the Congregation of Bishops and Regulars, in reply to a series of questions from the Congregation of the Oblates of Mary, declared that bishops were not to impede members of the secular clergy from entering this institute, even though the institute professed only simple vows.[4]

On January 25, 1848, the decree *Romani Pontificis* was issued by the Sacred Congregation of Bishops and Regulars. It defined the procedure to be followed in the accepting of candidates for the religious life. This decree applied to all religious orders and congregations of men. Among other things the superiors were required to obtain testimonials from the ordinary of the place of origin of the candidate, as well as from the ordinaries of those places where the candidate had lived for more than a year after the completion of his fifteenth year.[5] In obtaining the information for these testimonials the ordinaries were to inquire diligently into the qualities of the candidates. The testimonial letter was to include information on the age, the habits, the reputation, the condition, and the education of the candidate, and likewise was to reveal whether the candidate was affected with any censures,

---

[3] Const. *Quamvis iusto,* 30 apr. 1749, § 17—*Fontes,* n. 398.

[4] Bizzarri, *Collectanea,* p. 474.

[5] Bizzarri, *Collectanea,* pp. 831–832.

irregularities, or other canonical impediments, whether the candidate was in debt, and whether he was obliged to carry on the administration of another's property. The ordinary who issued the letter was under strict obligation to the truth, and was not permitted to refuse to give this information when it was requested of him.[6]

The Sacred Congregation of Bishops and Regulars through its various "*animadversiones*" with reference to constitutions submitted to it for approval indicated the provisions that were to be included in the constitutions for the sake of defining the bishop's rights and duties in the matter of the admission of candidates as well as of the dismissal of the professed subjects. Thus, while the superioress general could not act independently of the bishop in the reception of postulants, the permission of the bishop was necessary not only for the postulants' reception of the habit but also for the novices' admission to the first vows.[7] Dispensations from the vows taken in the religious congregations of women could be granted only by the Holy See. The superioress general and her consultors had no power to expel any sister without first consulting the bishop and the Apostolic See.[8] In a particularly grave case the bishop could dismiss a member of an institute of women, but he was then obliged to refer the matter to the Holy See for its approval.[9]

From these responses of the Sacred Congregation of Bishops and Regulars it is clear that the bishops were to supervise the admission of candidates to the reception of the habit, and of novices to their first profession of vows, in order to certify the presence of the necessary freedom on their part in the important step they were to take. In very grave cases there was acknowledged for the bishops the added right of dismissing a woman religious; but upon doing so there remained for them the obligation of referring the matter to the Holy See for approval. No such powers were given to the bishops over religious congregations of men.

---

[6] Bizzarri, *Collectanea,* p. 833.

[7] Bizzarri, *Collectanea,* pp. 775, 778.

[8] Bizzarri, *Collectanea,* pp. 779, 780, 781, 782, 783, 786, 788, 789.

[9] Bizzarri, *op. cit.,* p. 784.

Article 3. Legislation immediately Preceding the Code

Leo XII in his Constitution *Conditae a Christo,* in which he gave to institutes whose members were professed with simple vows a juridical character in the written law of the Church, defined at the same time the powers of the bishop over institutes of diocesan and pontifical approval. In the episcopally approved religious congregations of women the bishop was to be informed of the reception of novices or also of their first profession of vows, in order that he might ascertain the due freedom and qualifications of the aspirants. Only then could they be admitted to the novitiate or to the profession of vows.[10]

The bishop also had the power in such institutes to dismiss the professed and to dispense them from their vows, whether perpetual or temporary, with the exception of the perpetual vow of chastity. Due regard, however, was to be shown for the rights of the superioress general, especially when she justly dissented from such action.[11]

In pontifically approved religious congregations of women the bishop retained the right of examining the candidates before the reception of the habit and the profession of vows.[12] It remained, however, the exclusive right of the Holy See to dispense from the vows, whether perpetual or temporal.[13]

This right of the Holy See was qualified in 1911, when to the bishop there was acknowledged the right to expel a nun or a sister in cases of grave external scandal. Even in these cases, however, the confirmation of the Holy See had to be obtained without delay.[14] Thus the Constitution *Conditae a Christo* (December 8, 1900) together with the mentioned change remained, till the promulgation of the Code, the law of the Church in determining the rights of the bishop in this matter.

---

[10] Const. *Conditae a Christo,* § I, n. VII—*Fontes,* n. 644.

[11] *Ibid.,* § I, n. VIII.

[12] *Ibid.,* § II, n. 1.

[13] *Ibid.,* § II, n. II.

[14] S. C. de Religiosis, decr., 16 maii 1911—*AAS,* III (1911), 235.

CHAPTER VIII

RIGHTS OF THE BISHOP IN RELATION TO THE ADMINISTRATION OF TEMPORAL GOODS

Article 1. The Council of Trent

In monasteries and orders of men the administration of the temporal goods belonged to the officials thereof, who were removable at the will of their superiors.[1] The Council of Trent made no explicit mention of temporal administration with reference to the monasteries of nuns, but it seems that these monasteries were subject in this matter either to the regular superiors or to the bishop in his capacity of a delegate of the Holy See, for the same monasteries of nuns were subject to the regular superiors or to the bishop in the matter of visitation.[2]

The bishop's rights over the monasteries of nuns were clarified and extended in 1622 by Gregory XV (1621–1623) in the Constitution *Inscrutabili.* Through this enactment all the monasteries of nuns, even those which were subject to regulars, were made subject to the local ordinary in temporal as well as in spiritual matters. The local ordinary, acting as the delegate of the Holy See, had the right to receive from each convent in his diocese a yearly report on the administration of their temporal affairs. In cases of maladministration the bishop could impose suitable penalties.[3]

Article 2. The Eighteenth and the Nineteenth Centuries

At first there existed no explicit law dealing with the respective rights of the bishop and the religious congregations of men and women. It seems, however, that in the congregations of women, if they were founded by the bishops, the administration of the

[1] Sess. XXV, *de regularibus,* c. 2.

[2] Sess. XXV, *de regularibus,* c. 9.

[3] Const. *Inscrutabili,* 5 febr. 1622, § 5—*Fontes,* n. 199.

temporal goods was under the control of the bishops. The early religious congregations of women were completely subject to the local ordinary, and the superioress general was responsible to the bishop as her immediate superior. This is clear from the Constitution *Quamvis iusto* of Benedict XIV (1740–1758), in which the congregations of women professed with simple vows were indeed given recognition, but in a manner that left them under the ultimate control of the bishop.[4]

In the nineteenth century the Sacred Congregation of Bishops and Regulars did not furnish its approval for the constitutions of religious congregations, unless the constitutions first provided for the obtaining of permission from the Holy See in the matter of the alienation of property and the incurring of debts.[5] The constitutions had to provide also for the sending of a report on the administration of property to the Holy See every three years.[6]

In a dispute between the Bishop of Nancy and the Sisters of the Good Shepherd over temporal administration, it was decided by the Sacred Congregation of Bishops and Regulars that, though the institute had to render an account to the bishop, the temporal administration itself belonged to the superioress general, and not to the bishop.[7]

Article 3. Legislation immediately Preceding the Code

The Constitution *Conditae a Christo* more accurately defined the rights of the bishop in reference to the administration of the temporal goods. Thus, for religious congregations of diocesan approval the ordinary had the right to inspect, especially at the time of visitation, the entire administration of the temporal goods of the religious houses within his diocese.[8]

In the congregations of pontifical approval the administration of the temporal goods was entirely in the hands of the congrega-

[4] Const. *Quamvis iusto,* 30 apr. 1749—*Fontes,* n. 398.

[5] Bizzarri, *Collectanea,* pp. 781, 784, 787, 790, 793.

[6] Bizzarri, *ibid.,* pp. 793, 794.

[7] S. C. Ep. et Reg., *in causa Nanceven.,* 27 mart. 1896—*Analecta Ecclesiastica* (originally *Analecta Juris Pontificii,* Romae, 1855–1869; Parisiis, 1872–1891; *Analecta Ecclesiastica,* Romae, 1893–1911), IV (1896), 156.

[8] Const. *Conditae a Christo,* 8 dec. 1900—*Fontes,* n. 644.

tion itself, and only in the case of funds which were given for the purpose of public benefit in that place, or for the purpose of divine worship, did the bishop have any right of inspection.[9]

In response to a series of questions the Sacred Congregation for the Propagation of the Faith declared in 1903 that the permission of the Holy See was necessary for the alienation of the goods of any congregation of men or women, whether of pontifical or diocesan approval. The bishop, however, could exercise for the benefit of the said congregations, within the limits granted him, any privileges he possessed from the Holy See for the alienation of diocesan property.[10]

In 1906 a decree of the Sacred Congregation of Bishops and Regulars required superiors and superioresses general to answer a set form of questions, among which were included questions on the administration of the temporal goods.[11]

In 1909 the Sacred Congregation for Religious issued an Instruction on the administration and alienation of property, in which Instruction the congregations of diocesan approval were forbidden to incur any notable debts without the permission in writing of the bishop.[12] The contracting of debts in an amount beyond 10,000 lire ($2,000.00) required in addition the permission of the Holy See.[13]

Following this Instruction there was no further legislation on this matter until the promulgation of the Code.

---

[9] *Ibid.*, § II, n. IX.

[10] Resp. a S. Cong. de Propaganda Fide Archiepiscopo Milwauckiensi datum 15 ian. 1903—Vermeersch, *Supplementa,* p. 403.

[11] S. C. Ep. et Reg., decr. 16 iul. 1906—*Fontes,* n. 2052.

[12] Instr. *Inter ea,* 30 iul. 1909, n. I—*Fontes,* n. 4394.

[13] *Ibid.*, n. II—*Fontes,* n. 4394.

PART II

CANONICAL COMMENTARY

CHAPTER IX

THE FOUNDATION AND THE SUPPRESSION OF THE CONGREGATION, THE PROVINCE AND THE HOUSE

Article 1. The Foundation of the Congregation

In the history of the Church each age has seen men and women, inspired by God, raise up religious institutes to meet the needs of the times. These men and women did not actually establish the religious institutes; rather they were called by God to propose such institutes for the approval of ecclesiastical authority. Such is the case even today.[1] No religious institute can be canonically established without the approbation of the Church,[2] which approbation, according to the more common opinion, is required by the divine law itself.[3]

The Code, following the legislation of Leo XIII (1878–1903)[4] and that of Pius X (1903–1914),[5] gives to residential bishops the power to establish religious congregations of diocesan approval, but it explicitly excludes the vicar capitular and the vicar general.[6] The bishop however may exercise this right only after consulta-

[1] Fanfani, *De Iure Religiosorum ad Normam Codicis Iuris Canonici* (2. ed., Taurini-Romae: Ex Officina Libraria Marietti, 1925), p. 15 (hereinafter cited *De Iure Religiosorum*).

[2] *Religio est "societas, a legitima ecclesiastica auctoritate approbata . . ."*—Canon 488, n. 1.

[3] Fanfani, *De Iure Religiosorum,* p. 16. The two principal arguments presented for this view are: first, that to have a true religious institute it is necessary that the vows be accepted in the name of God, and only the Church itself can do this; secondly, that the vows of poverty and obedience in order that they constitute the true religious state require the authority of a prelate possessing spiritual power emanating from Christ. This is not possible except through the medium of and with the approbation of the Church.

[4] Const. *Conditae a Christo,* 8 dec. 1900, *Fontes,* n. 644.

[5] Motu proprio *Dei Providentis,* 16 iul. 1906—*Fontes,* n. 675.

[6] Canon 492, § 1.

tion with the Holy See.[7] Although the consultation with and the permission of the Holy See is not required, so it seems, for the validity of the foundation, the Holy See could later void a foundation made without its permission.[8] Included in the term residential bishops are all local ordinaries who have the same power as residential bishops, namely abbots and prelates *nullius,* vicars and prefects apostolic, and permanent apostolic administrators.[9]

Besides consultation with the Holy See, a second requisite is enjoined on bishops who establish tertiaries living in common. In such cases the tertiary group must be affiliated with the first order by its superior general.[10] It will be the bishop's duty in such cases to ascertain that this requirement of the law has been fulfilled. Such affiliation with the first Order does not lessen in any degree the tertiary's dependence upon the bishop.[11]

Consultation with the Holy See is the duty of the bishop, and not of the proposed religious institute, and his obligation in this respect has been made more explicit and detailed through the issuance of two decrees by the Sacred Congregation of Religious.[12] In the *Normae* of 1921 is contained the matter upon which the Holy See is to be informed before it will grant permission to the bishop to erect a religious institute. Thus the bishop is to report to the Holy See on the character of the author of the new congregation, the reason for its foundation, its name or title, the

---

[7] Canon 492, § 1.

[8] Larraona, "Commentarium Codicis" *CpR,* V (1924), 48; Coronata, *Institutiones Iuris Canonici ad Usum Utriusque Cleri et Scholarum* (2. ed., 5 vols., Taurini: Ex Officina Libraria Marietti, 1939–1947), I, 626 (hereafter cited *Institutiones*).

[9] Maroto, "Annotationes"—*CpR,* IV (1923), 197, VI.

[10] Canon 492, § 1.

[11] Fanfani, *De Iure Religiosorum,* p. 18.

[12] *Normae secundum quas S. Cong. de Religiosis in novis approbandis procedere solet,* 6 mart. 1921 (Romae: Typis Polyglottis Vaticanis, 1922), (hereafter cited *Normae* of 1921); cf. *AAS,* XIII (1921), 312–319; *Decretum circa Congregationes religiosas aut Pias Societates Iuris Dioecesani,* 30 nov. 1922—*AAS,* XIV (1922), 644–646. The Sacred Congregation for the Propagation of the Faith also issued an Instruction for the guidance of bishops in missionary territory: *Pro Religiosis Mulierum Institutis, ad Tuendam Puerorum Matrumque Vitam in locis Missionum,* 11 febr. 1936—*AAS,* XXVIII (1936), 208–209.

form, color and material of the habit to be worn by novices and professed, the number and type of works the congregation intends to assume, how it is to be supported, and finally whether or not there are other similar congregations in the diocese and, if so, what their activities are.[13]

The Holy See does not approve congregations which have no certain and proper purpose, save perhaps in missionary territory.[14] Nor does the Holy See readily approve congregations of women, when the nature of their work would expose them to scandals or grave moral dangers. An example of such would be an institute founded to nurse the sick in their homes day and night. On those occasions when for just reasons the Holy See does approve such institutes, it is required that there be sufficient precautions and safeguards in the constitutions against such scandals and dangers.[15] When the Holy See has granted its permission, then the bishop, either personally or through a delegate, to establish the new institute must issue a formal decree, whereupon the new congregation acquires juridical personality.[16] The formal decree of establishment is to be executed in writing, one copy to be kept in the archives of the diocese, and the other in the archives of the congregation.[17]

Following the formal establishment, the bishop must send to the Holy See a report in which is contained the precise title and scope of the foundation as well as a copy of the decree of establishment.[18]

A religious congregation is thus formally constituted in the eyes of the Church, becoming a true society, possessing juridical

---

[13] *Normae* of 1921, nn. 3–4.

[14] *Normae* of 1921, n. 13.

[15] *Normae* of 1921, n. 15.

[16] S. C. de Religiosis, decr. 30 nov. 1922—*AAS*, XIV (1922), 644, 646. The vicar general, even with a special mandate, would not be competent to establish a congregation, unless so delegated by the bishop. *Cf.* Larraona, "Commentarium Codicis"—*CpR*, V (1924), 43. The formal decree is not necessary for the valid erection of the Institute.—Orth, *The Approbation of Religious Institutes*, p. 111.

[17] Canon 375; S. C. de Religiosis, decr. 30 nov. 1922—*AAS*, XIV, (1922), 644.

[18] S. C. de Religiosis, decr. 30 nov. 1922—*AAS*, XIV (1922), 644.

moral personality with all the rights and obligations accorded to similar institutes within the framework of the common law.[19] An institute so established is of diocesan approval, and, even though in the course of time it spreads into many other dioceses, it remains such until it receives the decree of praise or the decree of approval from the Holy See. During this period it is fully subject to the jurisdiction of the local ordinary.[20] It is by reason of this subjection that the local ordinary's consent is required in order that the congregation may be extended into other dioceses.[21]

The nature of this complete subjection to the local ordinary will be shown in ensuing chapters, but it can be noted here that this does not signify that the local ordinary has complete power over the external and internal government of the institute, but rather that he has complete jurisdictional power over the institute according to the law. The institute, possessing as it does juridical personality, has the right to govern its own internal affairs.[22]

Once the institute has been canonically established, it is immediately subject to the law of the Code and its own constitutions in the administration of its internal and external affairs. It will therefore be the duty of the local ordinary to see that in this administration the requirements of canon law are carried out. Such an obligation presents difficulties, inasmuch as complete adherence to the law of the Code will not be possible in every instance by an institute newly founded.

One of the first duties of the institute subsequent to its establishment will be to provide for the election of officers to govern the institute. In the absence of any special provisions from the Sacred Congregation of Religious, the local ordinary would not be permitted to appoint the superior general or any of the other officers. Neither would he have the power to confirm in office the person acting as superior general or any of the other officers. Neither would he have the power to confirm in office the person acting as superior of the group previous to the canonical foundation. Rather, provision must be made for an election to be held

---

[19] Canon 100.

[20] Canon 492, § 2.

[21] Maroto, "Annotationes"—*CpR,* II (1921), 325.

[22] Canon 101, § 1; Bastien, *Directoire Canonique,* p. 39.

as soon as possible with strict adherence to the law of the Code and the constitutions. Yet, a dispensation from one or the other requirement would be necessary for an election so early in the life of the congregation.[23]

It is possible also that the institute in the judgment of the local ordinary is not sufficiently stable and developed to choose its own superiors. In such a case the local ordinary would again need special permission from the Holy See to appoint for a period of years the superior general and other major superiors. In reference to these superiors he would also need faculties to dispense from the requirements of the Code as to the age qualification and the requisite number of years spent as a professed religious.

Provision must also be made for the establishment of a canonical novitiate together with the appointment of a qualified and competent novice master in accordance with the constitutions and the Code.[24] It will not be possible in the beginning to appoint from among the members of the institute a novice master who possesses all the qualifications demanded by the law.[25] To appoint one in whom there are not fulfilled all the requirements of the common law, a dispensation is necessary from the Sacred Congregation of Religious.[26] It is permissible, and perhaps it is the better arrangement, that a religious of another institute should serve as novice master during the early years of the institute until such time as a member of the congregation is qualified to fill this position. Such a religious would need the permission of his own superiors, who in turn would need the permission of the Sacred Congregation of Religious, to allow him to remain outside his religious house for a period of time longer than six months.[27]

---

[23] While the local ordinary could grant dispensations from the requirements of the constitutions which treat of the rights of electing and of being elected for office, a dispensation from the requirements of the Code can be granted solely by the Holy See, v.g. the requirement enacted in Canon 504, namely that a candidate for the office of superior general must be professed ten years.

[24] Canon 554.

[25] Canon 559. The novice master, for example, must be professed for at least ten years.

[26] Canon 251, § 3.

[27] Canon 606.

Those engaged in the work of the institute as well as the superiors will not be able to make their novitiate immediately. In such cases it seems that some provision must be made for these members in order that they may be considered capable of holding office and of performing the work of the congregation without having made a canonical novitiate or profession of vows. The Sacred Congregation of Religious could possibly grant them permission to postpone their novitiate training for a time; or those who have already spent a number of years in the practice of the common religious life could be permitted to take temporary or perpetual vows in abstraction from the necessity of a formal novitiate.

From the above mentioned difficulties it is clear that the mere permission of the Holy See to found a congregation is not in itself sufficient for the valid, stable and efficient administration of a new congregation. Since such difficulties as those outlined above must be met by every new congregation at its inception, it seems to be the proper procedure for the local ordinary to foresee these difficulties and to place, together with his request for the permission to found a new institute, another request for extraordinary faculties, in order that he may properly cope with each of the possible situations that are likely to arise in connection with the effort to make such an institute canonically operative.

Thus, for example, he could request permission to admit to public vows, either perpetual or temporary, all those who have lived the common life for a certain specified number of years. If he deemed it necessary, he could seek permission either to appoint the superior general and his counsel for a period of years, or to confirm in office the author of the institute, or finally, in case of an election, to dispense the candidate from the Code's requirements relative to the age of the candidates and the number of years spent by them as professed religious. The local ordinary could also ask for the faculty to dispense from the requirements of the Code relative to the master of novices. Such a procedure as this would forestall any difficulties that might otherwise arise to hamper the progress of the congregation at its most critical stage. It would also dispel all possible future anxiety concerning either the validity of the vows taken by the members of the institute, or the acts of the officers of the congregation. It would preclude recourse at a later date to the Holy See for sanations, at least *ad cautelam,* for acts that were invalid from the beginning or at best only doubtfully valid.

Article 2. The Suppression of the Congregation

The moral personality of the diocese institute by its very nature gives the institute perpetuity. There are, however, two possible ways in which an institute can cease to exist, namely, through its inoperativeness for one hundred years, or through its suppression by the proper ecclesiastical authority.[28] In the first case, if, within the space of one hundred years the local ordinary wished to revive the institute, he could do so without recourse to the Holy See, even though there were no surviving members.[29]

The suppression of an institute can be effected either outright or through its union with another institute. In the second case, since the institute loses its moral personality through its union with another institute, this is equivalent to a total suppression, and the Holy See is alone competent to authorize it.[30] Even though there remain but one house of the institute, the Holy See alone can completely suppress a congregation of diocesan approval.[31]

In a case of the total suppression of an institute the Holy See reserves to itself the right to the disposition of the institute's property, preserving in each case the donor's wishes.[32] That the act of suppressing a religious institute is reserved to the Holy See represents a change in the law, for the pre-Code legislation gave to the bishops the right to suppress congregations of diocesan approval, provided that there were sufficiently grave reasons to warrant the act of suppression.[33] The bishop's sole obligation in this matter is to supply the Holy See with any information it seeks regarding the institute to be suppressed.

---

[28] Canon 102.

[29] Larraona, "Commentarium Codicis," *CpR,* V (1924), 257, nota 141; Coronata, *Institutiones,* I, 628, nota 3; Fanfani, *De Iure Religiosorum,* p. 25.

[30] Canon 493.

[31] Canon 493.

[32] Canon 493.

[33] Const. *Conditae a Christo,* § 1, n. VI—*Fontes,* n. 644.

The Holy See has nowhere given its reasons for reserving this right to itself, but its main reason seems to be, first, the fact that its permission was required for the establishment of such religious congregations; secondly, its desire to forestall all possibility of arbitrariness on the part of local ordinaries; and, finally, the possibility of conflicting opinions on the part of ordinaries when the institute in question extends into several dioceses.[34]

Article 3. The Foundation and the Suppression of Provinces

Although the Code makes no mention regarding the division of diocesan institutes into provinces, it cannot be therefore concluded that such a division is not permitted. Rather, such a division is possible; moreover, unlike the case of such a division for institutes of pontifical approval,[35] the intervention of the Holy See is not required.[36]

It is necessary, in order to determine what is required for the proper establishment and division of provinces within a congregation of diocesan approval, to consult the particular legislation as expressed in the constitutions of each such institute. If the constitutions either explicitly or implicitly treat of this matter, then these provisions must be observed.[37] In the event that the constitutions do not treat of this matter, then, inasmuch as the Code has not expressly legislated thereon, it is to be concluded by way of reliance on an analogous application of the law that for the valid erection of provinces there is required the consent of each ordinary in whose diocese any of the religious houses is situated, together with the consent of the local ordinary where the mother house is located.[38]

If the province to be erected embraces only one diocese, the consent of simply the local ordinary of that diocese is sufficient. If however the projected province embraces houses located in several dioceses, the consent of each of the local ordinaries in

---

[34] Bastien, *Directoire Canonique*, p. 47.

[35] Canon 494, § 1.

[36] Larraona, "Commentarium Codicis"—*CpR*, V (1924), 262.

[37] Larraona, "Commentarium Codicis"—*CpR*, V (1924), 262.

[38] Larraona, *loc. cit.*

question must be obtained.[39] A formal decree of the erection of the province is required, and this should be in writing.[40]

In the modification and suppression of provinces there is likewise required the permission of the local ordinary of the diocese where the mother house is located as well as of all the local ordinaries in whose dioceses any of the religious houses of the province are situated.[41]

In a case of the suppression or the extinction of a province the disposition of the goods of the province is to be made according to the constitutions. In the event that the constitutions do not treat this matter, then the ruling of canon 494, § 2, must be applied. That ruling reserves the disposition of the goods in such a case to the general chapter or, outside the time of the general chapter, to the superior general with his council, the laws of justice and the will of the donors being in each case duly observed. In no case, however, does the property of such a province accrue to a diocese. The property accrues to the institute itself, which exists within the same order and category of moral persons as the provinces of which the institute is composed.[42]

Article 4. The Foundation of Religious Houses

By the term " religious house " is meant here not the material building in which the religious live, but rather the religious community which makes up the collegiate moral personality.[43] A

---

[39] Larraona, *loc. cit.;* Vermeersch-Creusen, *Epitome Iuris Canonici cum Commentariis ad Scholas et ad Usum Privatum* (3 vols., Vol. I, altera editio, 1924, Mechliniae-Romae: H. Dessain), I, 312 (hereafter cited *Epitome*).

[40] Canon 100, § 1: Such a decree appears to be analogously called for as a result of the ruling contained in a decree of the Sacred Congregation of Religious, which required that the erection of the institute be effected by means of a formal written decree. Cf. S. C. de Religiosis, decr. 30 nov. 1922—*AAS,* XIV (1922), 644. Schäfer maintains that the requirement that the decree be in writing effects only the licitness of the action. Cf. *De Religiosis,* p. 123.

[41] Larraona, *ibid.,* p. 263, nota 167; Schäfer, *De Religiosis, loc. cit.*

[42] Larraona, *loc. cit.;* Schäfer, *loc. cit.*

[43] " Domus religiosa formaliter et proprio sensu in iure religiosorum significat religiosam communitatem. Et ubi adest propria communitas, habetur servatis servandis persona moralis collegialis."—Schäfer, *De Religiosis,* p. 61.

religious house can be either a formally developed or a juridically inchoate house (*domus formata aut non-formata*). A formally developed house is one in which there are assigned at least six professed members, of whom in a clerical institute four at least are priests.[44] A juridically inchoate house is one in which less than six professed members reside, or in which, if it is a clerical institute, less than four priests reside.[45] Even in a juridically inchoate house there must be at least three religious of the institute assigned, if the house is to be constituted as a moral person.[46]

As simultaneous with or in immediate consequence of the erection of the institute itself, the establishment of the first religious house of the institute, in accordance with all the requirements of law, is called for. This first house is known as the mother house. The local ordinary of the place wherein this first house is located acquires certain special rights and duties towards the institute as a result of the presence in his diocese of the mother house of the institute.[47]

Once an institute of diocesan approval is legitimately established, it possesses the power to found religious houses, but it can exercise this power only with the permission of the ordinary of the place where the mother house is located together with the permission of the ordinary in whose diocese the new house is to be established.[48] The permission of the bishop should be obtained in writing,[49] and the formal decree of establishment should be made in writing by the institute or by the province according to the constitutions.[50] It is to be noted, however, that the moral per-

[44] Canon 488, 5o.

[45] Canon 488, 5o.

[46] Canon 100, § 2.

[47] Larraona, "Commentarium Codicis"—*CpR,* V (1924), 327.

[48] Canon 495, § 1.

[49] Fanfani, *De Iure Religiosorum,* p. 29.

[50] Coronata, *Institutiones,* I, 632; canon 100, § 1, and analogously S. C. de Religiosis, decr., 30 nov. 1922—*AAS,* XIV (1922), 644. Larraona denies the absolute necessity of a formal decree.—Cf. "Commentarium Codicis," —*CpR,* V (1924), 418. While it is not necessary for the validity of the foundation, such a formal decree of erection will serve as proof that the house has been properly established.—Cf. Flanagan, *The Canonical Erection of Religious Houses,* p. 35.

sonality of the newly established religious house is only indirectly derived from the decree of the erection, and directly from the law itself, for the direct granting of the status of moral personality involves an act of jurisdiction of which diocesan institutes are not possessed.[51]

If the religious house is to be established in a territory subject to the Sacred Congregation for the Propagation of the Faith, the latter's permission is also required.[52] Some commentators maintain however that, if the house is to be established in a mission territory is to be used almost exclusively for the care of souls, and is completely subject to the local ordinary, then probably the permission of the Holy See is not required, since then there is not intended the foundation of a religious house in the true and proper sense.[53]

While Canon 497, § 2, admits of the possibility of limitations placed by the local ordinary on the scope and activities of a particular religious house to be established, provided these limitations do not conflict with the common law,[54] nevertheless, the permission granted by the local ordinary to erect a religious house is not to be considered either temporary or revocable at his will.[55] Before granting permission for the establishment of a religious house, the local ordinary is in duty bound to exercise a prudent judgment whether or not adequate provision exists for the sustenance of the house and its members from some reasonably secure source of revenue.[56] The local ordinary is also authorized to

[51] Larraona, "Commentarium Codicis"—*CpR,* V (1924), 418.

[52] Canon 497, § 1.

[53] Coronata, *Institutiones,* I, 635; Vermeersch, "Quaesita Varia," *Periodica de Re Canonica et Morali Utili praesertim Religiosis et Missionariis* (Brugis, 1905–1927), XII (1923), (2) (hereafter cited *Periodica*).

[54] Canon 497, § 2—Constituendae novae domus permissio facultatem secumfert pro religionibus clericalibus habendi ecclesiam vel publicum oratorium domui adnexum, salvo praescripto can. 1162, § 4, et sacra ministeria peragendi, servatis de iure servandis; pro omnibus religionibus, pia opera exercendi religionis propria, salvis conditionibus in ipsa permissione appositis.

[55] Larraona, "Commentarium Codicis"—*CpR,* VI (1925), 180.

[56] Canon 496. While this condition is certainly an important one, its fulfillment is not necessary for the valid establishment of the religious house.—Schäfer, *De Religiosis,* p. 133.

secure the fulfillment of the other two conditions for the valid and licit establishment of the religious house, namely the assignment of at least three religious to the house,[57] as well as the actual foundation of the house through the formal decree.[58]

Once there is accomplished the formal establishment of the religious house, the latter acquires a juridical collegiate personality. If it is a house of a clerical institute, it acquires also the right to have a church or a public oratory connected with it.[59] The local ordinary in such a case can restrict this right by granting permission for the public oratory only.[60] The local ordinary has also the right at least by negative action to determine the particular place in which the public oratory will be built, and thus he also has, at least indirectly, a determining power regarding the location of the religious house in any particular place.[61]

Once established the religious house has the right to engage in the pious work proper to its institute, subject always to the provisions and conditions contained in the permission of the local ordinary.[62] But a lay institute of diocesan approval requires a special permission from the local ordinary for the erection of even a semi-public oratory.[63]

A religious institute wishing to expand into a diocese other than the one in which the mother house is located, must have the permission not only of the local ordinary in whose diocese the institute is establishing a new foundation, but also the permission

---

[57] Canon 100, § 2.

[58] Canon 100, § 1. "Ne autem in re tam gravis momenti ullum dubium oriri possit et de legitimitate eiusdem personalitatis jugiter constare queat, sapienter per can. 100, § 1, praescribitur, ut personae morales (exceptis Ecclesia Catholica et Apostolica Sede) nonnisi per formale decretum a competente ecclesiastico Superiore erigi valeant."—S. C. de Religiosis, decr. 30 nov. 1922—*AAS,* XIV (1922), 644.

[59] Canon 497, § 2.

[60] Lynch, *Contracts between Bishops and Religious Congregations,* The Catholic University of America Canon Law Studies, n. 239 (Washington, D. C.: The Catholic University of America Press, 1946), p. 113.

[61] Canon 1162, § 4; Coronata, *Institutiones,* I, 636; Schäfer, *De Religiosis,* p. 135.

[62] Canon 497, § 2.

[63] Canon 1192, § 1; Schäfer, *De Religiosis,* p. 135.

of the local ordinary of the diocese of the mother house.[64] The local ordinary of the diocese of the mother house should not refuse permission for such an expansion, save for a grave cause.[65] Such a case would be the institute's lack of sufficient members to carry on its proper work in the new diocese while doing justice to its work in the diocese of the mother house, or the existence of a financial condition which would not permit such a division.[66] After the establishment of the first house in a second diocese the permission of the local ordinary of the diocese of the mother house is no longer required for the further expansion in the second diocese; the permission of the ordinary of the place where the expansion is undertaken will then suffice.[67]

Article 5. The Alteration of the Religious House

The alteration of a religious house may be of three types: simply a change in the material buildings, or a change in the external form of the house, or a change in the internal form of the house. A change in the material buildings is permissible without the consent of the local ordinary,[68] provided that the proposed alterations are not contrary to the conditions contained in the permission granted by the local ordinary,[69] or to the wishes and intentions of the donor, if the religious house had been given for some specific purpose.[70]

---

64 Canon 495, § 1.

65 Canon 495, § 1. Such an expansion on the part of an already existing institute is preferred by the Holy See to the establishment of a new institute to do similar work. Cf. const. *Conditae a Christo,* 1, n. 3—*Fontes,* n. 644.

66 Augustine, *A Commentary on the New Code of Canon Law,* III, 81.

67 Coronata, *Institutiones,* I, 634; Schäfer, De Religiosis, p. 131; Creusen-Ellis-Garesché, *Religious Men and Women in the Code* (4. English ed., Milwaukee: Bruce Publishing Co., 1940), p. 28.

68 Coronata, *Institutiones,* I, 638. There does not seem to be required a new permission for the re-opening of a house which either freely or through force has been allowed to become abandoned, provided that one hundred years had not elapsed since it was deserted. But even this last condition would not be necessary in the case of a forced desertion.—Goyeneche, " Consultationes," *CpR,* VII (1926), 394.

69 Canon 497, § 4.

70 Canon 1517. The Holy See alone is competent to give the necessary

Formal change in a religious house may be either internal or external. Formal changes which concern and touch only the internal order are possible without a new consent of the local ordinary, provided such changes be not contrary to the constitutions or the conditions stipulated by the local ordinary when he approved the foundation.[71] For a formal external change, namely one which exercises some external influence on the clergy or laity, the same formalities are required as for the erection of a new foundation, inasmuch as such a change is in fact the equivalent of a new foundation.[72]

Article 6. The Transfer of Religious Houses

With reference to the transfer of a religious house from one place to another, consideration must first be given both to the original permission of the local ordinary in consequence of which the house was founded, and also to the will of the donor if the latter manifested some specific wish regarding that point. Any restrictions or stipulations contained in the permission of the local ordinary or expressed by the will of the donor, whether implicit or explicit, must be strictly fulfilled.[73] The transfer of a house will also to some degree be restricted in view of the location of the public oratory or the church when either of these is connected with the religious house, since the location of both requires the special permission of the local ordinary.[74]

In the absence of any of the foregoing restrictive conditions, there still remains the problem of determining the distance a religious house may be moved before the transfer becomes the equivalent of a new foundation. Authors are in disagreement as

---

permission to change the last will of the donor, unless such a right was expressly granted to the local ordinary by the donor.

[71] Canon 497, § 4. The changing of a house for postulants to a house for students or for novices exemplifies such a formal internal change.

[72] Canon 497, § 4; Coronata, *Institutiones,* I, 638. If the house is in a territory subject to the Sacred Congregation for the Propagation of the Faith, a new permission of the latter is also necessary.—Augustine, *A Commentary on the New Code of Canon Law,* III, 93.

[73] Larraona, " Commentarium Codicis "—*CpR,* V (1924), 419.

[74] Canon 1162, § 4.

to what really constitutes a transfer of this type. Certainly a transfer of a house from one diocese to another, no matter how short the distance, would be the equivalent of a new foundation. Relative to a transfer within the diocese the more common opinion maintains that a transfer within the same city or village is permissible without any additional permission of the local ordinary.[75] Fanfani holds that a transfer of more than three miles is equivalent to a new foundation.[76] Schäfer holds a stricter view. He deems the granting of permission to be necessary, similarly as for a new foundation, when the house is transferred from the original site.[77]

Larraona presents sound arguments for holding the opinion that a transfer within the same city would not require a new permission.[78] Pre-Code legislation forbade the transfer of a religious house from one place to another.[79] The term *locus* was understood by pre-Code canonists to mean a city or a village. Thus a transfer within the city did not require a new permission of the local ordinary.[80] The Holy See, according to Larraona,[81] approved the practice of transferring religious houses within the city of Rome without additional permission. He notes also that the preparatory texts of canon 497, § 1, contained the words "*ad erigendam vel transferendam domum religiosam,*" thus indicating that it was the intention at the time to require permission as for a new formal foundation in the transfer of religious houses. Relative to the point of transfer, the lack of its mention in the final text of the Code seems to indicate an opposite disposition in the law. An additional argument may be adduced from canon 6, n. 4, which requires adherence to the interpretation of the past law in those cases wherein it cannot clearly be established that the law of the Code differs from the past law.[82]

---

[75] Larraona, *loc. cit.;* Coronata, *Institutiones,* I, 638; Augustine, *A Commentary on the New Code of Canon Law,* III, 93.

[76] Fanfani, *De Iure Religiosorum,* p. 32.

[77] Schäfer, *De Religiosis,* p. 138.

[78] Larraona, "Commentarium Codicis"—*CpR,* V (1924), 420.

[79] Const. *Romanos Pontifices,* 8 maii 1881, § 22—*Fontes,* n. 582.

[80] Wernz, *Ius Decretalium,* III, n. 168; Vermeersch, *De Religiosis,* I, n. 115; Bouix, *De Jure Regularium,* I, 250.

[81] Larraona, *loc. cit.*

[82] Flanagan, *The Canonical Erection of Religious Houses,* p. 114.

It may be concluded therefore that, whenever the local ordinary has made no restrictions of any kind, implicit or explicit, in his permission, and provided that the will of the donor is not opposed to the transfer, a religious house may be transferred within the same city, town or village without a new permission of the local ordinary. In the event of some restricting clause in the contract, a transfer beyond the confines of the designated boundaries would require a new permission of the local ordinary.

The transfer of the mother house from one diocese to another would require the permission of the two local ordinaries involved; and the local ordinary of the diocese where the mother house is located could reasonably oppose any such change when it entails the loss of special rights and duties in relation to the institute.[83] For the same reason the local ordinary into whose diocese it is planned to transfer the mother house must also give his consent, since he thereby assumes towards the institute the special rights and duties relinquished by the first ordinary.[84]

Article 7. The Establishment of Edifices Separate from the House

Even after the establishment of a religious house in a diocese, the special permission of the local ordinary is necessary for the building or operating of a school, a hospice, or any other such edifice. This permission must be explicit and in writing.[85] Although the text of canon 497, § 3, seems to indicate that there is postulated both the building *and* the opening of any such edifice before the permission of the local ordinary becomes necessary, nevertheless it is sufficiently clear both from the context and from the purpose of the law that the words "*aedificentur et aperiantur*" are to be taken disjunctively.[86]

It is necessary now to determine the meaning of the phrase "any other edifice." Commentators, though not in agreement as to the exact meaning of the term, generally concede that it does

[83] Thus, for example, his permission is always required for the first foundation in any other diocese.

[84] Larraona, "Commentarium Codicis"—*CpR*, VI (1925), 327.

[85] Canon 497, § 3.

[86] Larraona, "Commentarium Codicis"—*CpR*, V (1924), 430.

not include summer villas or rest houses for the exclusive use of religious, since these are to be considered as mere secular houses.[87] By the term "edifice" the Code seems to include all buildings devoted to works which have an external influence on the clergy and the laity, and yet are not in the canonical sense of the term religious houses with an independent moral personality.[88]

Less clear are the authors on the meaning of the term "separated." Coronata [89] attaches to it a twofold meaning, namely a formal and a material concept. An edifice is formally, even though not materially, separated from the religious house, if the institute opens or begins a work not proper to the purpose of the institute as stated in the constitutions. In such a case the explicit permission of the local ordinary is required. A materially separate edifice, according to Coronata, is one which lies at a distance of about one-half mile or more from the religious house itself. According to this view, the erection of any edifice within a half mile of the religious house, provided that it carries out work that is proper to the institute, does not postulate the special permission of the local ordinary. An additional circumstance that must always be considered in such cases is the possibility in the original permission for the foundation of a condition which sets a restriction on the erection of separate edifices.

Fanfani [90] merely says that, as long as the edifice is materially or morally united to the religious house, no special permission is required. Augustine (1872–1943)[91] did not advert to the provision for a moral unity. He stated that "separated seems to imply that the buildings mentioned must be distinct from the religious house, so that they are not under one roof with the

---

87 ". . . grancia tamen proprie dicta, villa ad rusticandum, etc. inspici debet non ut vera domus religiosa sed ut possessio ad domus religiosam pertinens, pro qua obtinenda specialis ordinarii licentia non videtur requiri."—Maroto, "Annotationes"—*CpR,* V (1924), 431; Wernz-Vidal, *Ius Canonicum ad Codicis Normam Exactam* (7 vols. in 8, Romae: Apud Aedes Universitatis Gregorianae, 1923–1938), III, n. 72 (hereafter cited *Ius Canonicum*).

88 Blat, *Commentarium Textus Codicis Iuris Canonici* (5 vols. in 6, Romae, 1919–1927), II, 88 (hereafter cited *Commentarium*).

89 *Institutiones,* I. 637.

90 Fanfani, *De Iure Religiosorum,* p. 34.

91 Augustine, *A Commentary on the New Code of Canon Law,* III, 91.

latter, but form a distinct and independent entity, for instance for fire insurance or taxation. . . . They may be called separated or distinct even if connected by a covered hallway or corridor." Bouscaren-Ellis understand separate to mean "not on the same grounds."[92] Larraona[93] maintains that such an edifice must be one which is ruled directly or through delegation by the superior of the religious house and must also be within the same city or at least in the same diocese as the religious house and only a little distance from it, if it is to be considered as not postulating the local ordinary's permission for its erection.

It seems reasonable to say therefore that canon 497, § 3, refers to any edifice devoted to a work that will have external influence on the clergy or the laity, that will be directly or through delegation ruled by the superior of the religious house, and that is outside the property of the religious house. When the foregoing conditions are present, the special written permission of the local ordinary is required. No formal decree of erection is necessary, since there is no question here of the founding of an independent moral person.[94]

Article 8. The Suppression and the Extinction of Religious Houses

Just as the institute itself can lose its moral personality in two ways, namely by extinction and by suppression, so also the religious house can lose its moral personality in the same way.[95] Desertion of a house for a period of one hundred years would cause it to cease to exist as a moral personality.[96] Prior to the lapse of one hundred years the religious institute would have the right to re-establish the religious house, even though the material buildings had been deserted or even destroyed, and this without any new permission of the local ordinary.[97] In the case of an

---

[92] Bouscaren-Ellis, *Canon Law, a Text and Commentary* (Milwaukee, Bruce Publishing Co., 1946), p. 236.

[93] Larraona, "Commentarium Codicis"—*CpR,* V (1924), 432.

[94] Canon 100, § 1.

[95] Canon 102, § 1.

[96] Canon 102, § 1.

[97] "Non requiritur ergo venia hic praescripta Ordinarii nec Apostolicae

unjust expulsion from a religious house, Coronata[98] holds that a natural extinction would not take place even after one hundred years. In such matters, however, each individual case would have to be decided on its own merits.[99]

Formally developed and also judicially inchoate religious houses can be suppressed by the local ordinary, after he has given the superior general an opportunity to be heard,[100] and provided that the house to be suppressed is not the only house of the institute.[101] For the validity of the suppression it is indeed necessary but it also suffices that the local ordinary merely give the superior general an opportunity to present his views; he is nowise bound to accept or follow the advice or judgment offered by the superior general.[102] Since the suppression of a religious house is a serious affair, the local ordinary should not so proceed, save for serious and weighty reasons. In every case of suppression the institute has the right of recourse to the Holy See with suspensive effect.[103]

In the event of such a suppression, the goods of the religious house are to be disposed of according to the constitutions or, if the constitutions make no provision for such an eventuality, according to the rules stated in the Code.[104] The Code in canon 1501 provides that in the extinction of a moral person the goods of such a moral person belong to the immediately superior moral person, which in this case would be either the province or the institute itself.

Sedis ad huiusmodi domum restaurandam vel recuperandam, antequam ipsa iuridice per suppressionem vel extinctionem ad normam iuris (c. 102) perierit." —Larraona, "Commentarium Codicis"—*CpR,* V (1924), 419.

98 *Institutiones,* I, 638, note 1.

99 Goyeneche, "Consultationes"—*CpR,* VII (1926), 395. Goyeneche notes that it is the practice of the Curia in the solution of such cases to consider particularly the length of time during which the house was abandoned and the efforts made to seek re-establishment in the interim.

100 Canon 498.

101 Canon 498.

102 Canon 105, n. 1.

103 Canon 499.

104 Blat, *Commentarium,* I, n. 80.

CHAPTER X

THE GOVERNMENT OF THE INSTITUTE

Article 1. The Jurisdiction of the Local Ordinary

The government of the internal affairs of religious institutes of diocesan approval belongs to the superiors and chapters of the institutes according to the norms of the constitutions and the ruling of the general law.[1] These officials govern the institute through the dominative power which they possess over the members of the congregation.[2]

Local ordinaries, on the other hand, rule by means of the power of jurisdiction those who are under them. In its fulness this power of jurisdiction resides in the Roman Pontiff. In a lesser degree it resides also in the local ordinaries. While the religious of diocesan approval owe first obedience to the Holy Father, their highest superior, to whom they are also bound by the vow of obedience,[3] they are also fully subject to the jurisdiction of the local ordinary according to the norm of the law.[4] Thus religious institutes of diocesan approval enjoy no exemption from the jurisdictional power of the local ordinary. The same canon, however, which places institutes of diocesan approval under the jurisdictional power of the local ordinary, also indicates that he is to use this power in only those instances in which its use is vindicated for him in the law.[5]

Accordingly superiors general and their chapters are not under the jurisdiction of the local ordinary relative to their acts of

[1] Canon 501, § 1.

[2] Canon 501, § 1.

[3] Canon 499, § 1.

[4] Canon 492, § 2.

[5] "Congregatio iuris dioecesani, quamvis decursu temporis in plures dioeceses diffusa, usque tamen dum pontificiae approbationis aut laudis testimonio caruerit, remanet dioecesana, Ordinariorum iurisdictioni ad normam iuris plane subiecta."—Canon 492, § 2.

government, save in those instances with regard to which such power is explicitly granted to him by the law of the Code or by the constitutions of the institute, for the institute, even though diocesan, possesses a moral juridical personality by reason of the formal decree of erection, and thus also possesses the right to its own internal life, its own internal field of action, its own internal authority, and its own activity in all that concerns its internal government.[6]

Some authors maintain that the local ordinary does possess dominative power over religious of diocesan approval, and accordingly can command such religious by reason of the vow of obedience.[7] The Code, however, nowhere speaks of the possession of this power by the local ordinaries, and the assumption of such power by one outside the institute itself seems to be contrary to the independent and autonomous nature of the institute. Furthermore, since it was felt necessary to indicate expressly in the Code the fact that the Roman Pontiff (as the institute's highest superior) can command in virtue of the vow of obedience,[8] it does not seem proper to acknowledge an identical power to local ordinaries apart from an express mention of such a grant in the

---

[6] Bastien, *Directoire Canonique*, p. 39. "Nimirum illa subiectio congregationum religiosarum iuris dioecesani ad ordinarios locorum non sit nimis urgenda, nec ita omnibus modis plena et absoluta dicenda, prout prima fronte alicui forsan videretur esse. E contra tenendum est potius ipsis congregationibus religiosis iuris dioecesani competere ius libere agendi in pluribus negotiis propriae vitae internae; nam, quamvis eiusmodi congregationes dicantur esse plane subiectae ordinariorum iurisdictioni (can. 492, § 2), sed ibi adiicitur quoque comma maxime attendendum, id est ad normam iuris; ius autem in pluribus favet et assistit hisce congregationibus, non solum propter ipsam naturam personae moralis collegialis quae in iure ipso agnoscitur, sed etiam propter plures ac maximi momenti postivas praescriptiones, quae in ipso iure communi habentur statutae. Quocirca huiusmodi congregationes ita revera sunt dicendae et habendae iuris dioecesani ut iam aliquam initialem participationem iuris pontificii prae se ferant."—Maroto, "Annotationes"—*CpR*, II (1921), 329.

[7] Coronata, *Institutiones*, I, 644; Fanfani, *De Iure Regularium*, p. 55; "Ordinarius loci gaudet religionibus iuris dioecesani potestate iurisdictionis et dominativa; etiam vi voti obedientiae in iis rebus, quae sunt e regula et constitutionibus praecipere potest."—Schäfer, *De Religiosis*, p. 159.

[8] Canon 499, § 1.

Code. Those who hold the view, namely, that the local ordinary can command in virtue of the vow of obedience, can neither sustain this claim by means of any authentic documents, nor can they clearly deduce it from the intrinsic nature of congregations of diocesan approval.[9]

The power of the local ordinary is therefore one of jurisdiction. It is in fact nothing less than the jurisdiction which he possesses over the rest of the diocese, but it is limited and defined by the law of the Code and the particular constitutions of each institute, so that the local ordinary can claim no jurisdiction over an institute in any particular matter unless it can be clearly established in the Code that he possesses such jurisdiction.

Article 2. Elections

The Code, in following the previous legislation, makes no provision for the presence of the local ordinary at the election of the superior general of institutes of men religious of diocesan approval.

Canon 506, § 4, however, gives the local ordinary definite rights and duties in relation to the election of the superioress general in congregations of women religious of diocesan approval.[10] Higher superiors are generally elected by the chapter of the religious institute according to the common law,[11] and in intimate conformity with the constitutions of the institute, provided that these do not reflect any opposition to the law of the Code. Such chapters of religious institutes of diocesan approval are chapters in the

---

[9] "*Haec doctrina documentis authenticis non confirmatur nec clare ex natura intrinseca congregationis dioecesanae deducitur.*"—Larraona, "Commentarium Codicis"—*Cpr,* VI (1925), 182, note 74 (italics inserted). Berutti admits such a possibility if the constitutions of a particular institute expressly indicate that the local ordinaries have such power, or if the religious in the actual profession of the vow of obedience expressly promise such obedience to the local ordinaries; in every other case he denies the possibility.—Berutti, *Institutiones Iuris Canonici* (6 vols., Vol. III, Taurini-Romae; Marietti, 1936), III, 48 (hereinafter cited *Institutiones*).

[10] The local ordinary has the right to preside at the election of the superioress general only, and not at the election of the councilors general and other lesser officers. Cf. Berutti, *Institutiones,* III, 60.

[11] Canon 507, § 1.

canonical sense of the term, and therefore are subject to the rulings contained in canons 160–182.[12]

It is the duty of the superioress general to call the chapter to meeting and to indicate the place where it is to be held. She may choose a place outside the diocese of the mother house, if the institute has spread to other dioceses.[13] The ordinary of the place where the election is held has the duty to preside at the election of the superioress general in congregations of diocesan approval with the right to confirm or to veto the choice of the electors according to the dictates of his conscience.[14]

It is therefore the duty of the superioress general or whoever is in charge of the institute to inform the ordinary of the place where the election is to be held, and to do this sufficiently in advance of the pending election to enable him to make plans to be present either personally or by delegate.[15]

At the election, the local ordinary presides with the power of jurisdiction, and not merely with a specific mark of honor.[16] On him falls the responsibility for a valid and a licit election, for his is the duty to direct and govern the act of the election. He has the authority to settle practical questions of law that may arise, to impose penances if necessary and, in general, to exercise all discretionary powers.[17] He may dispense from a requirement of

[12] Creusen-Garesché-Ellis, *Religious Men and Women in the Code*, p. 51; Larraona, "Commentarium Codicis"—*CpR*, VIII (1927), 108.

[13] S. C. de Religiosis, resp., 17 iul. 1921—*AAS*, XIII (1921), 481. Schäfer maintains that the constitutions may reserve this to the ordinary of the place where the mother house is situated.—*De Religiosis*, p. 212.

[14] Canon 506, § 4. Cf. also S. C. de Religiosis, resp., 17 iul. 1921—*AAS*, XIII (1921), 481. This response indicates clearly that in the event the election is held outside the diocese of the mother house, the ordinary of the place where the election is held presides.

[15] Canon 506, § 4. Larraona notes the fact that, since the ordinary confessor of nuns is forbidden in canon 506, § 3, to act as teller, it also seems forbidden him to act as delegate of the ordinary.—" Commentarium Codicis" —*CpR*, VIII (1927), 24, note 334.

[16] P. C. I., 30 iul. 1934—*AAS*, XXVI (1934), 494. The election would be invalid without his presence.—Larraona, "Commentarium Codicis"—*CpR*, VIII (1927), 105.

[17] Parsons, *Canonical Elections*, The Catholic University of America

the constitutions of the institute,[18] but not from the general law unless he possesses a special indult, save in a case of necessity, and then only when the specified conditions as set forth in canon 81 are duly verified.

He does not have the right to appoint priests as tellers, but rather these are to be chosen from among members of the chapter.[19]

If a candidate has received an absolute majority in the first or second balloting, or a relative majority in the third, the duty then devolves upon the local ordinary to confirm or to veto the choice according to the dictates of his conscience. In the event that he confirms the choice of the electors, he is to sign the record of the election together with the notary and the tellers, and the record is to be preserved in the archives of the institute.[20] The confirmation should be made by means of a formal written decree.[21] If for some just and grave cause the local ordinary feels obliged to annul the election, then the election is to be repeated with the aid of even a fourth balloting if this be necessary, provided of course the constitutions permit the utilization of a fourth ballot.[22]

The problem which presents itself in the event of a tie vote on the last ballot centers about the power of the local ordinary to break the tie. Canon 101, § 1, n. 1, gives to the presiding officer of the chapter the right to break a tie by his vote. Some authors maintain that in virtue of this canon the local ordinary, as the presiding officer, can break such a tie.[23]

Canon Law Studies, n. 118 (Washington, D. C.; The Catholic University of America Press, 1939), p. 135.

[18] Creusen-Garesché-Ellis, *Religious Men and Women in the Code,* p. 61.

[19] Creusen-Garesché-Ellis, *op. cit.,* p. 55.

[20] Canon 171, § 5.

[21] Canon 177, § 3.

[22] Parsons, *Canonical Elections,* p. 155. Berutti (*Institutiones,* III, p. 61) notes that the Sacred Congregation of Religious in approving new constitutions of institutes of women is wont to require that a provision be made in them that, if in the third balloting the election of the superioress general is not achieved because of the lack of a requisite majority, a fourth and last balloting shall take place in which only those religious shall be eligible for election who in the third balloting received the greater number of votes.

[23] Coronata, *Institutiones,* I, 660; Larraona, "Commentarium Codicis"—*CpR,* VIII (1927), 22; Vermeersch-Creusen, *Epitome,* I, 323.

However not all the authors are agreed on this matter. The question centers about canon 101. Does it presuppose that the presiding officer is a member of the chapter with the right to vote? The canon indeed seems to imply that, since it speaks of his vote as being the deciding one. Yet, if such be the case, then the local ordinary would have no right to break the tie, since he does not possess a vote.[24]

Michiels brings into question the meaning of *suo voto,* which he maintains means " by his own decision " and not " by his own vote." The word use for vote in the Code, he states, is *suffragium.*[25] Since the point is a disputed one, the necessitated interpretation in the matter seems to be the interpretation which was favored in the earlier law.[26] In the pre-Code law the local ordinary was forbidden to break such a tie.[27] Such, then, seems to be the better interpretation of the canon.[28] In such a case, if the electors refused to cede to the local ordinary their right of election, the local ordinary should refer the matter to the Sacred Congregation of Religious.

In two cases the right to name the superioress general belongs to the ordinary of the place where the election should have been held. The first case is failure by the chapter to elect a candidate within the time specified by the Code.[29] The second case occurs when the chapter has been deprived of the right of election by way of punishment for some crime.[30]

---

[24] Chelodi, *Ius de Personis,* p. 422, nota 4.

[25] Michiels, *Principia Generalia de Personis in Ecclesia* (Lublin in Polonia, 1932), p. 390.

[26] Canon 6, n. 4.

[27] Ferraris, Lucius, *Prompta Bibliotheca Canonica, Iuridica, Moralis, Theologica necnon Ascetica, Polemica, Rubricistica, et Historica* (8 vols., Romae, 1885–1892; *Supplementum,* ed. Ianuarius Bucceroni, Romae, 1889), s. v. *Abbatissa,* nn. 29–30, and the decisions of the Sacred Congregations there cited.

[28] Parsons, *Canonical Elections,* p. 155.

[29] Canon 161 calls for an election to be held within three months after the vacancy of the office.

[30] Canon 178; Creusen-Garesché-Ellis, *Religious Men and Women in the Code,* pp. 58–59.

CHAPTER XI

CANONICAL VISITATION

ARTICLE 1. THE DUTY OF THE LOCAL ORDINARY

The local ordinary has the duty within every five-year period to visit each house of the various congregations of diocesan approval located in his diocese. This duty he can fulfill himself personally or through a delegate.[1] In the event that the local ordinary does appoint a delegate to perform this task, the latter's power should be clearly indicated in writing. Such a delegate may be appointed even though the local ordinary could without any difficulty conduct the visitation personally.[2] Directors appointed by the local ordinary to aid institutes of women in their relations with the diocese do not by the fact of this appointment receive the powers of visitators. Such power must be expressly given to them.[3]

The local ordinary has the right to take with him two companions who are clerics. But it seems more in keeping with the paternal spirit that should characterize the visitation, if the local ordinary conducts the act of visitation without being at the time accompanied by others, unless it were a case of judicial procedure.[4]

Blat [5] and Toso [6] deny that the vicar capitular has the power to visit diocesan religious institutes. Their argument is based on the wording of canon 315, § 2, n. 1, which indicates the power of the temporary administrator of a diocese. This canon grants to

---

[1] Canon 512, § 1, n. 2.

[2] Coronata, *Institutiones,* I, 667.

[3] Goyeneche, "Quaenam sunt attributiones Directoris Congregationis dioecesanae?"—*CpR,* XIV (1933), 357.

[4] Augustine, *A Commentary on the New Code of Canon Law,* III, 141; Coronata, *Institutiones,* I, 668.

[5] Blat, *Commentarium,* II, n. 333.

[6] Toso, *Commentaria Minora,* III, 137.

the temporary administrator the same rights and duties as the vicar capitular, but adds, "*sed sede plena, potest dioecesim visitare ad tramitem iuris.*" This could seem to indicate that an additional power, not possessed by the vicar capitular, is here granted to the temporary administrator. Inasmuch however as the vicar capitular receives the ordinary episcopal jurisdiction with the exception of the things which are expressly prohibited,[7] and inasmuch as the Code does not expressly prohibit to the vicar capitular the exercise of the jurisdiction here in question, precisely because the prohibition remains so doubtful in its character, the power to conduct a visitation appears to belong to the vicar capitular.[8]

The local ordinary cannot dispense himself from this important duty of visitation.[9] When he is himself unable to make the visitation at the stated time, he should appoint a delegate to act in his stead. While the law does not provide for a more frequent visitation, the local ordinary would have the right and even the duty to conduct a visitation more frequently if some grave scandal or disorder called for his act of instituting a visitation as a means of allaying the scandal or quelling the disorder.[10]

If the local ordinary fails in his duty to conduct the requisite visitations of the religious institutes established in his diocese, it is then the duty of the metropolitan to inform the Holy See and to conduct the visitation after having received the approval of the Holy See. Throughout the period of the visitation the metropolitan would have the power to preach, to hear confessions, to absolve from the episcopally reserved cases, to inquire about the life and character of the clerics, to denounce infamous clerics to the local ordinary for punishment, and personally to punish even with censures the notorious offenses committed against himself or his attendants.[11]

---

[7] "Sicut ad Capitulum ante deputationem Vicarii Capitularis, ita deinde ad Vicarium Capitularem transit ordinaria Episcopi iurisdictio in spiritualibus et temporalibus, exceptis iis quae in iure expresse sunt eidem prohibita." Canon 435, § 1.

[8] Reilly, *The Visitation of Religious,* p. 86.

[9] Larraona, "Commentarium Codicis"—*CpR,* VIII (1927), 441.

[10] Reilly, *The Visitation of Religious,* p. 87.

[11] Canon 274, n. 5.

Article 2. The Nature of the Visitation

Canon 343, § 1, delineates the purpose of the local ordinary's visitation of his diocese. Its purpose is to preserve sound doctrine, to safeguard morals, to correct abuses, to promote peace, virtue, piety, and discipline, and properly to order all other affairs that serve the promoting of religion. Since institutes of diocesan approval are completely under the local ordinary's jurisdiction, he will conduct his visitation of these institutes with a view to accomplishing the purposes outlined here. He will be concerned in general, therefore, with the matters that concern the fulfillment of the purpose of the religious institute, the observance of discipline, and the financial condition of the various houses of the congregation.[12]

In particular the local ordinary or his delegate will concern himself with visiting the church or the oratory and its sacristy for the purpose of examining the vestments and sacred vessels.[13] His inquiry will also include the confessionals.[14] It will be his duty to ascertain whether or not the sacraments of penance and of the Holy Eucharist are being received according to the prescriptions of the Code,[15] the instructions of the Holy See [16] and the particular requirements of the constitutions, provided that these are not contrary to the Code. Other matters subject to this visitation are the observance of the prescriptions of the constitutions and of the vows, the attendance at the spiritual exercises, the observance of the law of enclosure, and the administration of the property and the goods belonging to houses of the institute.[17]

The local ordinary has the right and the duty of questioning any of the religious whom he judges it desirable to hear, and the

---

[12] Bastien, *Directoire Canonique,* p. 82.

[13] Canon 1261.

[14] Canons 909; 910.

[15] Canon 595, § 1, n. 3; § 2.

[16] S. C. de Sacramentis: Instructio reservata. De Communione habituali et pene generali in Seminariis, Collegiis, Communitatibus etiam religiosis et de abusibus in eadem praecavendis,—Larraona, "Annotationes"—*CpRM,* XXI (1940), 133.

[17] Augustine, *A Commentary on the New Code of Canon Law,* III, 138.

religious are under obligation to answer all inquiries truthfully.[18] Superiors may not in any way prevent their subjects from fulfilling this obligation, nor may they in any other way hinder the scope of the visitation.[19] Superiors and others who impede the visitation are liable to the punishment of ineligibility for office, and in the case of superiors to deprivation of the office itself.[20]

Ordinarily the visitor will proceed in a paternal rather than in a coercive manner, and only in extraordinary cases should he find it necessary to have recourse to judicial procedure and the use of canonical penalties.[21] If he finds it necessary to proceed in this way, then the visitor may require the members of the institute to take an oath to the truth of their statements.[22]

If in the course of the visitation the local ordinary finds any lapse or any infringement of the law which is of a nature serious enough to demand correction, he should not hesitate to take the proper measures needed for the correction, proceeding even here however in a fatherly way, unless the nature of the offense is so serious as to demand recourse to judicial procedure.[23] Thus if a religious has committed a crime which is serious or gravely scandalous, the local ordinary could exercise coercive power and inflict canonical penalties and remedies.[24]

The visitation itself should not be drawn out over a long period of time, but should end as quickly as efficiency will permit. To observe the demands of courtesy and to permit the proper and necessary preparations to be made in advance, the local ordinary

[18] Canon 513, § 1.

[19] Canon 513, § 1.

[20] Canon 2413, §§ 1, 2.

[21] Augustine, *A Commentary on the New Code of Canon Law,* III, 139.

[22] Canon 1944, § 1; Fanfani, *De Iure Religiosorum,* p. 83. They can also be given a command to keep secret the matters discussed with the visitator.

[23] Creusen-Garesché-Ellis, *Religious Men and Women in the Code,* p. 69. In the event of such a judicial procedure, an appeal against the sentence will suspend its effect; in the case of a paternal procedure, the recourse does not have any suspensive effect.—Cf. Canon 513, § 2.

[24] Augustine, *A Commentary on the New Code of Canon Law,* III, 139; Bastien, *Directoire Canonique,* p. 83.

should inform the institute of the proposed visitation, or at least make it at regular known intervals.[25]

Throughout the visitation, and especially in the imposing of decrees, the local ordinary should proceed with caution. He should duly guard against compromising or attenuating the dominative power of the various superiors of the institute. Great prudence and moderation should distinguish the local ordinary in this matter.[26] He should be careful to preserve the unity of the institutes through the preservation of its autonomy,[27] and accordingly should refrain from any unwarranted interference in purely internal matters of the institute and leave to the superiors the correction of minor infractions.[28]

Expenses incurred in the course of the visitation are to be defrayed according to legitimate custom. In no case however may the local ordinary or any of his companions accept donations for the visitation itself.[29]

ARTICLE 3. THE VISITATION OF THE MOTHER HOUSE

The term " mother house " as used in this article refers to the house where the superior general or the provincial general and his staff reside.[30] In an institute of women religious it is at the mother house that the dowry funds are administered by the institute.[31] To the local ordinary of the mother house falls the duty of carefully watching over the administration of these dowry funds, and especially at the time of the visitation he should examine the funds and their administration.[32] The examination should include the dowries of both the novices and the professed.[33] At the time of the visitation the local ordinary should determine

---

25 Augustine, *ibid.*, p. 135.

26 Larraona, " Commentarium Codicis "—*CpR,* V (1924), 144, nota 94.

27 Maroto, " Annotationes "—*CpR,* II (1921), 323.

28 Larraona, " Commentarium Codicis "—*CpR,* V (1924), 144.

29 Canon 346.

30 Canon 508 imposes on all superiors of religious the obligation of residence, each in the proper house of the congregation.

31 Canon 550, § 1.

32 Canon 550, § 2.

33 Larraona, " Commentarium Codicis "—*CpR,* XIV (1933), 350.

whether or not all the dowries of the professed religious are properly invested, and whether or not his consent had been first obtained for each investment.[34]

This duty and right belongs to the local ordinary in whose diocese the mother house is located.[35] Schäfer maintains, however, that the local ordinary here concerned is the ordinary of the place where each religious lives. Thus he requires that the superioress general send to each local ordinary an account of the administration of the dowry funds of each religious residing in his diocese.[36] Such an opinion does not seem admissible in view of the fact that canon 2412, n. 1, grants to the local ordinary concerned the right to punish, even to the extent of deprivation of office, superioresses general who, in violation of canon 549, presume in any way to spend the dowry funds. The only local ordinary who could inflict such penalties would be he who has jurisdiction over the superioresses, namely the local ordinary of the diocese where the mother house is located. Furthermore, the local ordinary is to exact an accounting of the dowry funds at the time of the visitation,[37] and the only one who could make such a demand of a superioress on the occasion of a visitation is the ordinary of the place where the mother house is located, i.e., where the superioress resides.[38]

A far more important question, however, in relation to the local ordinary's power of visitation concerns the extent of his right of visitation in relation to the mother house as such. Is the superior general or the provincial and his staff subject to the visitation of the local ordinary in whose diocese they reside?[39] In answer, a distinction can and must be made between the local superior of the mother house with his subjects and the general curia with its council. The local ordinary has the right to visit the local su-

---

[34] Canon 549.

[35] Coronata, *Institutiones,* I, 706.

[36] Schäfer, *De Religiosis,* p. 288.

[37] Canon 550, § 2.

[38] Reilly, *The Visitation of Religious,* pp. 92–93.

[39] Canon 512, § 1, reads: "Ordinarius loci per se vel per alium quinto quoque anno visitare debet: . . . n. 2. "Singulas domos sive virorum sive mulierum Congregationis iuris dioecesani."

perior, the latter's administration and his subjects. There is no doubt either that, if the congregation is confined to the one diocese, the local ordinary has the right of visitation over the entire institute, together with all its temporal affairs.[40]

In the event that the institute extends into several dioceses, it is not easy to establish the view that the local ordinary retains this same right of visitation over the general curia and its administration. Reilly,[41] following for the most part the arguments of D'Ambrosio (1885–1945),[42] holds the view that the local ordinary does possess the power to visit the general curia. He argues that, since the local ordinary is given the right to visit the mother house, "this should be taken to mean the entire house: *ubi lex non distinguit nec nos distinguere debemus.* If a distinction is to be introduced between the general curia and the rest of the community, there must be clear and compelling reasons for so doing." [43]

He holds indeed that there is no reason for making such a distinction. Yet he does state that such a distinction can be made,[44] and there do seem to be compelling reasons for so distinguishing between the general curia and mother house as a religious house. For when the local ordinary assumes the right to conduct a visitation of the general or provincial curia, he is then conducting a visitation of the institute or province, and not merely a visitation of the mother house. He will then be concerning himself with matters that extend beyond the limitations of his diocese and which concern the institute as a whole.

The argument advanced, namely, that so to exempt diocesan congregations from such a visitation would place them in a more favorable position than congregations of pontifical approval, who must submit quinquennial reports to the Holy See,[45] does not seem to justify an extension of the term "religious house" to include

---

[40] Reilly, *The Visitation of Religious,* p. 93.

[41] *The Visitation of Religious,* pp. 94–97.

[42] "De Domo Generalitia Instituti Polydioecesani quoad Canonicam Visitationem can. 512, §1, n. 2 praescriptam, et quoad poenas can. 2413 sancitas"—*Apollinaris* (Romae, 1928–), I (1928), 417–422.

[43] Reilly, *op. cit.,* p. 94.

[44] Reilly, *op. cit.,* p. 93.

[45] Canon 510.

"province or institute." Provision can and should be made for the canonical visitation of such institutes. As Larraona states,[46] such vigilance belongs to the local ordinaries, but not to one exclusively, but to all collectively in whose diocese the institute or the province has houses. This norm applies to all those things which are common to the institute as a whole, and which exceed the limits of any one diocese. There is nothing which forbids the local ordinary of the diocese where the mother house is situated from acting as the delegate of all the other local ordinaries in conducting the entire visitation in their name and stead. Thus such power could be granted in the constitutions to the local ordinary of the diocese of the mother house.[47]

D'Ambrosio presented another argument which seems scarcely acceptable, since it was based in part on reasons which, at the most, are true in only exceptional cases.[48] He maintained that, since the local ordinary of the diocese of the mother house has the right to preside at the elections of the superior or superioress general and the assistants general with the right to confirm them, since it is he who directs the discussions of the general chapter and has a right to demand that an accounting of the administration and government of the curia be presented to the general

---

[46] "Commentarium Codicis"—*CpR,* XIV (1933), 416.

[47] Larraona admits the possibility of a tacit delegation, and in a case of necessity the possibility of a presumed delegation of the local ordinary of the mother house. In the case of a presumed delegation there must exist a clear and certain necessity; in the case of a tacit delegation the fact upon which the delegation is based must be definite and certain.—"Commentarium Codicis"—*CpR,* XIV (1933), 418, note 784.

[48] D'Ambrosio ("De Domo Generalitia Instituti Polydioecesani Quoad Canonicam Visitationem, can. 512, § 1, n. 2 praescriptam, et quoad poenas can. 2413 sancitas"—*Apollinaris,* I [1928], 420) wrote: "Praeterea si ad Ordinarium loci, in quo Generalitia Domus extat alicuius instituti polydioecesani, ad normam iuris pertinet praesidere Capitulo Generali in quo eliguntur et Superiorissa vel Superior Generalis et Adsistentes Generales nec non eos confirmare; si item ad Ordinarium loci pertinet eiusdem Capituli discussiones dirigere, et insuper exigere ut ad examen revocentur in actu capituli rationes generalis administrationis et regiminis Curiae quae mox est officio soluta, et tandem res omnes in ipsomet capitulo gestas sua auctoritate firmare, quae autem non posset vigilantiam et inspectionem in eamdem generalitiam Curiam extra generale capitulum exercere?"

chapter for examination, and since he has the right also to confirm by his own authority the matters considered in the general chapter, he should therefore be able to exercise vigilance and the right of inspection over the general curia outside the general chapter.

Yet, nowhere does the Code give to the local ordinary the right to preside at the election of the superior general and his assistants, or the right to confirm or to veto such elections. The local ordinary of the mother house can preside at the election of the superioress general, but only in the case in which the election is held in the diocese of the mother house; the superioress general, however, may choose for the general chapter a place outside the diocese of the mother house, in which case the ordinary of the place chosen has the right to preside at the election.[49] After the election of the new superioress general, she presides at the election of the other officers. In no case does the ordinary of the place where the election is held have the right to confirm or to veto the election of an officer other than the highest superior.[50]

Nowhere does the Code give a local ordinary the right to preside at or in any way to direct the discussions of the general chapter of a diocesan institute. Neither is it required that any of the acts of the chapter be submitted to him for approval, unless he has reserved this right to himself.[51] The only exceptional case wherein the local ordinary possesses such power is the case for which such power is expressly granted him in the constitutions of the institute.

Larraona[52] and Bastien (1866–1940)[53] maintained the view that the local ordinary of the mother house does not possess this power to visit the general curia. Larraona argued from the text and context of canon 512, and from analogous enactments both in the

---

[49] S. C. de Religiosis, resp. 2 iul. 1921—*AAS,* XIII (1921), 481.

[50] Parsons, *Canonical Elections,* p. 183.

[51] Ellis, " The General Chapter of Affairs in a Religious Congregation "—*Review for Religious* (St. Mary's, Kansas, 1942-), I, (1942), 258.

[52] " Commentarium Codicis "—*CpR,* XIV (1933), 416–418; Larraona, " De Visitatorum potestate applicandi poenas in can. 2413 statutas "—*CpR,* X (1929), 373–377.

[53] *Directoire Canonique,* n. 305.

present and in the past law. He noted that from the second half of the last century up to the Code itself the general rule militated against such an intervention in the government of the institute by any one local ordinary.[54] Rather the general principle seems to be that provision for the welfare of and vigilance over the diocesan institutes has come to be entrusted to all the local ordinaries in whose dioceses the institute has religious houses.[55] Thus for example, a projected change in the constitutions of an institute now requires the collective consent of the ordinaries of all the dioceses in which the institute has houses.[56]

The text of canon 512, § 2, n. 2, gives the local ordinary the right to conduct a visitation of all the *houses* of diocesan institutes established in his diocese and thus it does not seem that the term "house" comprises also the concept of the "province or institute." Furthermore, if in this instance the text is to be so interpreted as to include a visitation of the general curia, then is it to be so interpreted in § 2, n. 3, of the same canon, wherein the local ordinary is given the right and duty to visit houses of lay congregations of pontifical approval?

To grant to the local ordinary of the diocese of the mother house the power to conduct a visitation of the general curia does not seem just, since the institute and its government transcends diocesan limits, nor does it seem equitable to the other local ordinaries in whose dioceses the institute has houses. Indeed, it seems to work to the disadvantage of the institute itself, since the local ordinary would be more inclined to consider the interests of his own diocese, not perhaps to the exclusion of the good of the institute, but in preference to it.[57]

---

[54] Bizzarri, *Collectanea,* pp. 778, 779, 780; *Acta et Decreta Concilii Plenarii Americae Latinae,* n. 326. This council warned bishops not to assume with reference to religious institutes any powers which were not theirs, and to respect the jurisdiction of other bishops who had houses of the institute in their diocese.

[55] Larraona, "De Visitatorum potestate applicandi poenas in can. 2413 statutas"—*CpR,* X (1929), 374.

[56] Canon 495, § 2.

[57] Larraona, *ibid.,* p. 376. The response of the Sacred Congregation of Religious (July 2, 1921), which gave to the superioress general the right to determine the place of the general chapter, and thus also the right to

Therefore, while the mother house is subject to the visitation of the local ordinary in whose diocese it is located, it does not seem to be within the power of the local ordinary to include in his visitation the general curia, and this by reason of canon 512, § 1, n. 2. Rather, some other provision for this visitation should be made, either in the constitutions of the individual institutes, or through the collective consent of all the ordinaries in whose dioceses the institute has houses.[58]

---

determine the local ordinary who is to confirm the election, seems to be an indication of the desire of the Holy See to preserve the independence of such institutes from the will or the desire of any one individual local ordinary.—*AAS,* XIII (1921), 481.

[58] Since the completion of this dissertation, the Sacred Congregation of Religious has decreed that the superior general and superioress general of congregations of diocesan approval must submit every five years, a report on the condition of the congregation to the local ordinary of the diocese where the mother house is located. This report is to be made according to a form yet to be approved for such institutes and is to be signed by the superior general and his council. The ordinary of the place where the mother house is located, is to submit this report to all the ordinaries of other places where the institute is established. A copy of this report, signed by all the local ordinaries concerned, together with their own judgment concerning the institute, is to be forwarded to the Sacred Congregation of Religious within the year.—S. C. de Religiosis, decr., 9 iul. 1947—*AAS,* XL (1948), 379–380.

CHAPTER XII

ADMISSION AND DEPARTURE

ARTICLE 1. ADMISSION

The Church has always been solicitous to preserve the freedom of action of all its members. In order to safeguard this freedom, the Church declares that all acts performed by physical or moral persons as the result of an external force to which an effective resistance cannot be offered are to be regarded as if their performance had not been undertaken at all.[1] Especially true is this with reference to religious profession, for any profession of vows made as a result of violence, grave fear or substantial fraud is by that very fact invalid.[2]

It is for this reason, namely, to safeguard the freedom of choice of the candidate, that the Code requires the local ordinary to examine in congregations of women religious the dispositions of the candidates for temporary and perpetual vows, as well as of the candidates for the novitiate.[3] Thus a candidate for perpetual vows will have had the opportunity on three occasions to indicate to the local ordinary her true dispositions with reference to the religious life.[4] So seriously does the Church regard freedom in this matter that it punishes with an unreserved excommunication all, no matter what their rank may be, who in any way compel another to enter a religious institute or to make profession of vows in such an institute.[5]

---

[1] Canon 103, § 1.

[2] Canon 572, § 1, n. 4.

[3] Canon 522, § 2.

[4] If the religious makes more than one temporary profession, the local ordinary is not obliged to inquire into her dispositions before each temporary profession, but only at the first of them. Cf. Coronata, *Institutiones,* I, 729; Augustine, *A Commentary on the New Code of Canon Law,* III, 228; Vermeersch-Creusen, *Epitome,* I, 366.

[5] Canon 2352.

It is the duty of the religious superioress to inform the local ordinary at least two months in advance, whenever candidates are to be admitted to the novitiate, to their first temporary profession of vows, and to their perpetual profession of vows.[6] The religious superioress concerned is the one designated by the constitutions. In the event that the constitutions are silent in this matter, then the superioress general has the obligation of imposing this duty on some particular superioress or of fulfilling it herself.[7] This is a serious obligation and the local ordinary is empowered to punish according to the gravity of the guilt, even to the extent of deprivation of office, any superioress who fails in her duty in this regard.[8]

The local ordinary to be notified is he in whose diocese the candidate to be examined resides.[9] It is the duty of the local ordinary at least thirty days before the admission to the novitiate or the profession of vows to examine the candidate diligently as to whether she is free of coercion, is fully aware of what she is about to do, and is taking the steps with a pious and free intention.[10]

The local ordinary can therefore question the candidate about the essential nature and obligations of the vows and the constitutions.[11] Once satisfied that the candidate is fully acquainted with the step she is about to take, and that she is taking it with full freedom, he cannot oppose her admission to the novitiate or the profession. It then pertains to the superioress general with her council to decide whether or not the person may be permitted to enter the novitiate or make the profession of vows.[12]

While some authors permit the local ordinary to accept travel-

---

[6] Canon 552, § 1.

[7] Coronata, *Institutiones,* I, 728. Schäfer imposes the obligation on the superioress general or the superioress of the novitiate house.—*De Religiosis,* p. 393.

[8] Canon 2412.

[9] Schäfer, *loc. cit.;* Coronata, *ibid.,* p. 729.

[10] Canon 552, § 2.

[11] Bouscaren-Ellis, *Canon Law, A Text and Commentary,* p. 265.

[12] Vermeersch-Creusen, *Epitome,* I, 336; Schäfer, *loc. cit.;* Coronata, *Institutiones,* I, 729.

ing expenses, as incurred by reason of the examination he had to make, especially in the case of a long trip,[13] it seems more in accordance with the mind of the Holy See that he should not accept even traveling expenses.[14] In no case however may a fee be exacted for the examination, even though there be an immemorial custom in favor of such a practice.[15]

The local ordinary, if he is absent from the diocese or otherwise impeded, can delegate a priest to make this examination.[16] The obligation itself of making this examination is a grave one, and to omit it would constitute a serious transgression of the law.[17] Such an omission however would not render the subsequent profession invalid.[18]

Article 2. The Religious Profession

It is required for a valid religious profession that the profession be received by the legitimate superior, either personally or through a delegate, in accordance with the constitutions.[19] This is an exercise of dominative power [20] and as such is not reserved to the local ordinary. Rather, it is the right and duty of the superior and superioress to exercise this power in accordance with the constitutions.[21] In those cases however in which the constitutions designate the local ordinary to receive the profession, it is required for validity that he preside either personally or through

---

[13] Fanfani, *De Iure Religiosorum,* pp. 217–218; Bouscaren-Ellis, *Canon Law, A Text and Commentary,* p. 265.

[14] Coronata, *Institutiones,* I, 729.

[15] S. C. de Religiosis resp. ad dubium, 20 mart. 1922—*AAS,* XIV (1922), 352.

[16] Canon 552, § 2.

[17] Schäfer, *De Religiosis,* p. 393; Vermeersch-Creusen, *Epitome,* I, 366.

[18] Bastien, *Directoire Canonique,* p. 312.

[19] Canon 572, § 1, n. 6.

[20] Maroto, "Annotationes"—*CpR,* II (1921), 162–164; Fanfani, *De Iure Religiosorum,* 273.

[21] Maroto, *loc. cit.;* Schäfer, *De Religiosis,* p. 444; Fanfani, *De Iure Religiosorum,* p. 273. Augustine's opinion that the bishop of the diocese alone has this privilege seems scarcely tenable in the light of the wording of the canon and of the common doctrine of the canonists.—Cf. Augustine, *A Commentary on the New Code of Canon Law,* III, 257.

a delegate at the profession.[22] Yet, in receiving the vows, the local ordinary acts not in his own name, but in the name of the superioress, as having a legitimate mandate, for the reception of the religious profession is a duty reserved to the proper internal superior or superioress of the congregation.[23] The written document attesting to the fact of the profession is to be signed by the one receiving the profession.[24]

Article 3. Voluntary Departure from the Religious Life

The postulancy is a period of probation for the candidate. During this period the institute is able to study the suitableness of the candidate, and the candidate has an opportunity to become acquainted with the religious life and its obligations.[25]

During the period of probation the postulant is free to leave the institute at any time. In the case also of novices there is no canonical obligation that binds them to the institute, so that they are free to leave at any time during their novitiate.[26] A religious is likewise free from any canonical obligation to remain in the institute at the expiration of the temporary vows.[27] In each of these cases there is required no intervention of any kind on the part of the institute or of the local ordinary to make this departure effective.

In a case other than those just indicated, a religious must have an indult of exclaustration or secularization to leave the religious life either temporarily or permanently.[28] In institutes of diocesan approval such indults can be given by the local ordinary of the place where the religious lawfully resides.[29] An indult of exclaustration connotes permission to leave the institute temporarily,

---

[22] Bastien, *Directoire Canonique,* 346.

[23] P. C. I., 1 mart. 1921—*AAS,* XIII (1921), 177; Schäfer, *De Religiosis,* p. 444.

[24] Canon 576, § 2.

[25] Schäfer, *De Religiosis,* p. 352.

[26] Canon 571.

[27] Canon 637.

[28] Canon 639.

[29] Canon 638; P. C. I., 24 iul. 1939—*AAS,* XXXI (1939), 321.

while an indult of secularization implies a permission to leave the institute permanently.[30]

A religious, though for some just reason he must leave the institute for a time, remains a religious, and continues bound by the vows and the other obligations of the religious life which he can fulfill in the world. He may not, however, wear the religious habit;[31] moreover, he temporarily loses the right to cast a vote and to have others cast a vote for him as a candidate for office, but he retains all the purely spiritual privileges of the institute. During the period of his absence from the religious institute he remains a subject of the ordinary of the place where he resides, in place of being subject to his own proper superior. He is subject to the local ordinary in such a case by the vow of obedience.[32]

Secularization is the complete and final grant of separation from the institute at the request of the religious. In the case of a member of an institute of diocesan approval, this secularization can be granted by the ordinary of the place where the religious lawfully resides. It can be refused by the religious who requested it, even though in accordance with canon 56, the issued rescript has become executed by the superior general. If the superior, however, has grave reasons to the contrary, he should refer the entire matter to the Sacred Congregation for Religious.[33]

A religious thus secularized must put off the religious habit and conduct himself as a secular in all that pertains to the Mass, the Divine Office, and the use and the administration of the sacraments. He is no longer bound by the vows or any other obligations of the religious life, and if by apostolic indult such a one again enters the religious life, he must make a new novitiate, take vows again, and take his place among the professed according to the date of his new profession.[34]

---

[30] Canon 638.

[31] Canon 639; the Code Commission in a reply dated Nov. 12, 1922, did however acknowledge the power for local ordinaries in view of special reasons to allow an exclaustrated religious to wear the religious habit.—*AAS*, XIV (1922), 662.

[32] Canon 639.

[33] S. C. de Religiosis resp. ad dubium, 1 aug. 1922—*AAS*, XIV (1922), 501.

[34] Canon 640.

A religious in major orders, if he becomes secularized or if he leaves the institute at the end of the temporary vows, must return to his proper diocese, if he has not lost it through his perpetual profession[35] and his proper ordinary must receive him.[36] If the religious has lost his diocese through his perpetual profession, then he may not exercise his sacred orders outside the institute, until either he has found a bishop willing to receive him, or the Holy See has made some other provision.[37]

Since the local ordinary does possess the power to secularize religious of diocesan approval,[38] and since in the Code no restriction is placed on his right relative to the secularization of such religious who are in major orders, it seems that the local ordinary does possess the power to secularize such religious before they have obtained a benevolent bishop. But the manner in which this power is to be used by the local ordinary seems best indicated by the practice of the Holy See in similar instances. The Holy See is not wont to grant an indult of secularization until the religious in major orders has found a benevolent bishop, who will sufficiently provide for the religious.[39] Local ordinaries in like manner therefore are held to follow this practice, namely, to grant such indults only after the religious has found a benevolent bishop.[40]

A bishop may receive such a religious in one of two ways. He may receive him unconditionally, in which case the religious is incardinated automatically in the diocese, or he may receive him on trial for a period of three years, and, if he wishes, for a period of another three years.[41] After this six year period of trial, the cleric religious, who has not been dismissed by the bishop becomes automatically incardinated in the diocese.[42]

---

[35] Canon 585.

[36] Canon 641, § 1.

[37] Canon 641, § 1.

[38] Canon 638.

[39] Schäfer, *De Religiosis*, p. 736; Goyeneche, "Consultationes"—*CpR*, VI (1925), 91.

[40] Schäfer, *loc. cit.*

[41] Canon 642, § 2; this prorogation of time for a second three-year period can be tacit as well as expressed—P. C. I., 27 iul. 1942—*AAS*, XXXIV (1942), 241.

[42] Canon 642, § 2.

The vicar general can not grant the incardination without a special mandate, nor can the vicar capitular or the administrator of a diocese do so, until after the diocesan see has been vacant for a year, and then only with the consent of the chapter.[43]

ARTICLE 4. INVOLUNTARY DEPARTURE FROM THE RELIGIOUS LIFE

The religious institute for a just and reasonable cause may dismiss a religious in temporary vows, provided that the reason is not simply that of poor health, unless it can be certainly proved that the religious fraudulently hid or dissimulated such a condition.[44] A sufficient reason for the dismissal of one in temporary vows would be the evident lack of a religious vocation, or of the qualities necessary for carrying on the work of the institute, or of the due regard for religious discipline.[45]

In the case of all religious, whether under temporary or perpetual vows, a dismissal follows automatically in the three following cases: (1) that of a public apostasy from the Catholic faith, that is, of a complete abandonment of the Christian Faith;[46] (2) that in which a religious flees from his religious institute with a person of the other sex; and (3) that in which a religious contracts or attempts to contract marriage, even the so-called civil union.[47] The dismissal is not dependent on any declaration of the fact by the superior, but occurs automatically with the commission of the crime.[48] It is, however, the duty of the major superior to make together with his chapter or council according to the norms of the constitution a written declaration of the fact, and this together with the proof of the fact is to be preserved in the archives of the institute.[49]

In reference to institutes of diocesan approval, the local ordinary has the power to dismiss from the religious life any member in temporary vows residing in his diocese. This power, however,

---

[43] Schäfer, *De Religiosis*, p. 737.

[44] Canon 637.

[45] Augustine, *A Commentary on the New Code of Canon Law*, III, 371.

[46] Cf. Canon 1325, § 2.

[47] Canon 646, § 1, nn. 1, 2, 3.

[48] P. C. I., 30 iul. 1934—*AAS*, XXVI (1934), 494.

[49] Canon 646, § 2.

he should not use without the knowledge of or against the just opposition of the superior general.[50] In proceeding to dismiss such a religious the local ordinary is gravely bound in conscience to follow the conditions set down in the Code. While these conditions are not necessary for the validity of the dismissal,[51] the religious has the right of recourse to the Holy See, during which time the dismissal has no juridical effects. The religious has ten days, from the time at which he has become aware of his right, in which to make recourse to the Holy See.[52]

The reasons for the dismissal in such a case must be grave,[53] but the reasons can lie either on the side of the institute or on the side of the religious. The lack of a religious spirit is a sufficient reason, provided that repeated warnings together with salutary penances proved of no avail. In no case is poor health to be considered as a reason, unless it is clear that it was fraudulently hidden or dissimulated.[54]

The reasons for the dismissal must likewise be certain, although it is not necessary that they be proved by means of a formal judicial procedure. The proofs, however, should be gathered and recorded for forwarding to the Sacred Congregation for Religious in the event that a recourse is later instituted. The reasons should also be made known to the religious in order that he may be afforded an opportunity to answer them, and his answers are to be faithfully recorded in writing.[55]

After the decree of dismissal has been issued, the religious has the right of recourse to the Holy See with the effect that the decree of dismissal will in the meantime remain inoperative.[56] He can make his recourse directly by means of a letter to the

---

[50] Canon 647, § 1.

[51] Coronata, *Institutiones,* I, 868.

[52] Canon 647, § 2, n. 4; S. C. de Religiosis, declar., 20 iul. 1923—*AAS,* XV (1923), 457; Schäfer, *De Religiosis,* p. 762; Coronata, *Institutiones,* I, 869.

[53] Canon 647, § 2, n. 1.

[54] Canon 647, § 2, n. 2.

[55] Canon 647, § 2, n. 3.

[56] Canon 647, § 2, n. 4.

Sacred Congregation of Religious, or indirectly through the person who communicated the decree to him.[57]

If it is a woman religious who is to be dismissed, and she has been received without a dowry and is unable to provide for herself, charity demands that provision should be made by the congregation both for her safe return home and for her sustenance for such a period of time as is mutually agreed upon or determined by the local ordinary in the event of a lack of agreement between the dismissed religious and the institute.[58] A religious under temporary vows thus dismissed is free from all the obligations of the vows, but, if in major orders, retains of course all the obligations arising from the major orders. A religious in minor orders is by the very fact of his dismissal reduced to the lay state.[59]

When the religious to be dismissed is under perpetual vows, a distinction regarding the procedure must be made according as the religious belongs to a congregation of men religious or to a congregation of women religious. In congregations of men religious, when the institute starts the procedure for dismissal, the following steps must be taken before the local ordinary enters into the procedure. It is necessary outside the case of automatic dismissal that the religious commit three grave and external offenses, and after a twofold warning show no amendment,[60] before action can be taken for his dismissal. The offenses must be of

[57] S. C. de Religiosis, declar., 20 iul. 1923—*AAS,* XV (1924), 457. In order to forestall all possible later dispute in the matter, the Sacred Congregation noted in this declaration that it is expedient for the superior to inform the religious, in the very document that intimates his dismissal, of the latter's right to invoke a recourse, and of the time that is granted for this.

[58] Canon 647, § 2, n. 5. In the event that the dowry does not constitute a reasonably estimated charitable subsidy, the institute is bound to supply the amount which is wanting to make up a fitting charitable subsidy. Cf. S. C. de Religiosis resp., 2 mar. 1924—*AAS,* XVI (1925), 165.

[59] Canon 648.

[60] Canon 649. The word offense is taken here in the meaning of canon 2195, § 1, namely as an external and morally imputable violation of a law to which has been added at least an indeterminate canonical sanction. Schäfer, *De Religiosis,* p. 765, nota 3; Fanfani, *De Iure Religiosorum,* p. 503.

the same species or, if different, such that when taken together they manifest a perverse and obstinate will in evil. One continuous offense is sufficient if it perdures despite repeated warnings, so that virtually it can be considered equal to three offenses.[61] For the warranted issuance of a warning it is postulated that the offense be notorious, that it be manifest through an extra-judicial confession, or that it be known in consequence of other sufficient proofs which were the result of previous inquiry.[62] The warnings are to be given by the subject's immediate major superior, either personally or through a delegate who has been given the mandate of the superior, but only after he has obtained information required by canon 658. A mandate which authorizes the first warning holds also for the second.[63] The two warnings are to be given after the first two offenses. When the religious has persisted in a continuous offense, the first and second warnings are to be separated by at least two full days.[64]

Together with the warnings the superior should add opportune exhortations and corrections together with penances and other penal remedies, such as are considered suited to the amendment of the offender and the reparation of the scandal. Wherever possible the superior is to remove the occasions of such offenses, even to the extent of transferring the religious from one house to another, where vigilance will be easier and the occasion of sinning more remote.[65] The threat of dismissal is to accompany each warning.[66]

The religious is considered not to have amended his ways if after the second warning he commits a third offense or persists in the same one. After the third offense, six days must elapse before any further action can be taken.[67] Following this lapse of

[61] Canon 657.

[62] Canon 658, § 1. A crime is notorious when it is publicly known and when it was committed under such circumstances that no evasive method suffices to conceal it and no legal subterfuge avails to excuse it.—Canon 2197, § 2; Fanfani, *De Iure Religiosorum,* p. 503.

[63] Canon 659.

[64] Canon 660.

[65] Canon 661, §§ 1, 2.

[66] Canon 661, § 3.

[67] Canon 662.

time the superior general together with his council shall consider all the testimony in the case, and then vote whether or not the religious shall be dismissed.[68]

If the majority vote calls for the dismissal, then the entire matter with all the necessary proofs and documents shall be referred to the local ordinary where the religious resides. The local ordinary is then to decide according to his own prudent judgment on the dismissal of the religious.[69] The religious has the right to explain his actions and to answer all charges against him, and his defense is to be faithfully recorded in the documents of the case.[70]

In deciding such cases the local ordinary is given extensive power. He must not in view of his possession of this power consider himself exempt from a prudent investigation of each case. It is his duty, therefore, to investigate carefully all phases of the case before he reaches a decision.[71] The decree of dismissal issued by the local ordinary is not a judicial sentence, but an administrative decree, and against it the religious has the right to invoke a recourse to the Sacred Congregation for Religious with the effect that the decree remains inoperative while the recourse is pending. If the religious invokes a recourse, he must do so within ten days from the time that he became aware of the fact that a decree of dismissal was issued.[72]

In the event that a recourse is instituted, the pertinent documents then to be sent are to contain proof of the following facts: (1) the three grave external offenses; (2) the warnings which were repeated at least twice; (3) the incorrigibility of the religious; (4) his opportunity to defend himself; (5) his defense; (6) the vote of the council; and (7) the local ordinary's decree.[73]

---

[68] Canon 650, § 1. The vote of the council is of a definitive character. Berutti, *Institutiones,* III, 346.

[69] Canon 650, § 2, n. 1.

[70] Canon 650, § 3.

[71] Schäfer, *De Religiosis,* p. 758; Vermeersch, "Quaesita Varia"—*Periodica,* XII (1923–1924), (63).

[72] Coronata, *Institutiones,* I, 852; Fanfani, *De Iure Religiosorum,* p. 504; Schäfer, *De Religiosis,* p. 766.

[73] Schäfer, *De Religiosis,* p. 766. If the religious refuses to defend himself, it must be indicated in the acts that he was given this opportunity. Schäfer, *De Religiosis, loc. cit.*

In the dismissal of women religious who are under perpetual vows, it is not necessary that there be three grave external offenses; rather, the Code simply speaks of grave external causes together with incorrigibility.[74] It seems that the causes must be of such a nature as to be imputable to the religious, and that from a theological approach they reflect an imputability of a grave and serious character.[75] Vermeersch-Creusen hold that the causes which suffice for the dismissal of a woman religious who is in temporary vows prove sufficient also for her dismissal when she has taken perpetual vows. Thus a grave culpability would not be postulated.[76] This, however, seems rather severe, for the condition of a religious in temporary vows is less secure than the condition of a religious in perpetual vows. Chelodi (1880–1922)[77] required culpable external causes and a gravely serious breach of discipline.

The religious should be warned to correct the fault, and every effort should be made through suitable penances and corrections to amend the harm done and to remove the scandal caused by the delinquency. The warnings need not be strictly canonical, but they should be given in writing or in the presence of two witnesses so that proof of this fact will thus be made available for the acts of the case when these are presented to the local ordinary for his decision, or to the Holy See in the case of recourse against the decision.[78] It seems expedient in connection with the warning to add the threat of punishment or also the threat of dismissal, although this is not necessary.[79]

The religious must be given every opportunity to defend any of her actions. This means that she must be informed that cognizance has been taken of her actions, in order that she may thus be given a full opportunity to explain them. Her answers should be written down and then signed by her, or, if she refuses to sign the acts, this fact should be noted in the records.[80]

---

[74] Canon 651, § 1.

[75] Coronata, *Institutiones,* I, 872–873.

[76] *Epitome,* I, 450; Schäfer concurs in this opinion.—*De Religiosis,* p. 767.

[77] *Ius de Personis,* p. 486.

[78] Chelodi, *loc. cit.;* Schäfer, *De Religiosis,* p. 768.

[79] Schäfer, *De Religiosis,* p. 767, nota 5.

[80] Canon 657, § 2, n. 3.

The religious should be given a period of trial in which she has the opportunity to prove to the institute that she intends to amend her ways.[81] The Code does not indicate the length of time that the probation should take or in what it should consist. The time element is a matter to be decided in each particular case. As for the manner of conducting such a period of probation, it will be for each superioress to use whatever means she prudently deems adequate to bring about the correction of the religious. Thus worthwhile penances, exhortations, threats of punishment, and especially threats of dismissal, should prove effective.[82]

If, despite the warnings and the period of probation, the religious shows no signs that give hope of amendment, then the superioress general should gather all the necessary proofs and documents and, after consulting with her council,[83] should refer the entire matter to the ordinary of the place where the religious resides.[84] It remains then for the local ordinary to consider the case and to issue the decree of dismissal, if he sees fit.[85]

Through the local ordinary's decree the religious is dismissed from the institute. There is not required any confirmation by the Holy See.[86] The competent ordinary is not the local ordinary of the place where the mother house is located, but rather the ordinary of the place where the religious resides. Against the decree of dismissal the religious has the right of invoking a suspensive recourse to the Holy See.[87]

From the foregoing considerations it is clear that the local ordinary in reference to congregations of diocesan approval both of

---

81 Canon 651, § 1.

82 Coronata, *Institutiones,* I, 873; Schäfer, *De Religiosis,* p. 767. Although the Code does not state which superioress is competent in these matters, it seems to be the superioress general.—Coronata, *loc. cit.*

83 While the Code is silent on the matter of consultation with her council, it would seem best in a matter of so great import that she be guided by the vote of her council.—Coronata, *Institutiones,* I, 873; Schäfer, *De Religiosis,* p. 769.

84 Canons 651, § 2; 652.

85 Canon 652.

86 Schäfer, *De Religiosis,* p. 768.

87 Coronata, *Institutiones,* I, 875; Schäfer, *De Religiosis,* p. 768; Fanfani, *De Iure Religiosorum,* p. 513.

men and women religious possesses the definitive power of issuing a dismissal.[88] Since the local ordinary possesses this power, can he proceed against the religious who are perpetually professed, even without waiting for or depending on the prior instituting of action against the religious by the competent religious superiors of the institute? The Code[89] presupposes that normally any necessary action of this type will be instituted by the congregation. There does not seem, however, to be any limitation or prohibition of the power of the local ordinary that would prevent him by reason of his jurisdiction in this matter over the religious institutes of diocesan approval from starting action for the dismissal of a religious under perpetual vows.

Tabera[90] outlines the following arguments in favor of this view. In the Constitution *Conditae a Christo*,[91] which is the source for the legislation of the Code on matters pertaining to the dismissal of religious of diocesan institutes, the bishop possessed the right to dismiss religious under perpetual vows from such institutes, with the limitation that the right was not to be used without the knowledge of or against the just objections of the major superior or superioress of the institute. Canon 650, § 2, n. 1, gives the local ordinary the power to dismiss those who are under perpetual vows in accordance with his own prudent judgment, apart from the necessity of any other person's vote or opinion. It left therefore entirely to the local ordinary to decide for or against the dismissal. It seems therefore that the preparatory steps on the part of the institute, which steps are required when the action is begun by the institute, are not necessary if the local ordinary should institute the action in that he proceeds according to his own prudent judgment.

Furthermore, canon 650, § 2, n. 1, states that in the dismissal of a religious under perpetual vows the local ordinary is to adhere to the norm of canon 647. Canon 647, § 1, with reference to the case of a religious under perpetual vows seems to grant the local ordinary the right to dismiss such a religious through a use

---

[88] Canon 650, § 2, n. 1; Canon 652, § 1.

[89] Canon 650, § 1.

[90] " Studia Canonica "—*CpR*, XIII (1932), 115–126.

[91] § I, n. VIII—*Fontes*, n. 644.

of his own power, independently of any action by the institute, provided that he does not use this power without the knowledge of or against the just objections of the major superior, and provided that he has reasons for the dismissal which can be certainly proved.

Against such a dismissal, however, the religious would have the right of invoking a suspensive recourse to the Holy See. This right of recourse can scarcely be doubted, for even though the Code [92] does not mention this right explicitly with reference to the dismissal of religious under perpetual vows, it does mention this right implicitly when in canon 650, § 2, n. 1, which treats of the dismissal of those who are in perpetual vows, it appeals also to what is stated in canon 647, which canon in § 2, n. 4, vindicates the option of recourse to a religious who has taken but temporary vows. Since religious under temporary vows possess such a right, it cannot be denied to religious under perpetual vows.[93]

There must now be considered the mode of procedure in the more urgent cases, which of their nature call for immediate action for the sake of forestalling scandal or of preventing injury to the congregation. Such urgency is present in two cases: first, in a case of some grave external scandal, and secondly in a case of very imminent injury to the congregation.[94] The postulated injury may be either temporal or spiritual, as long as it affects the institute, the province or a religious house of the institute.[95]

Together with such scandal or injury, there is required a second necessary condition for the effecting of an immediate dismissal, namely, that the dismissal is the only means available for precluding either the scandal or the injury, or at least that such a dismissal will probably avert or at least notably lessen the scandal or injury.[96]

When these two conditions are present, proofs of the existence

[92] Canons 650 and 652.

[93] Canon 647, § 2, n. 4; Tabera, "Studia Canonica"—*CpR,* XIV (1933), 54-55.

[94] Canon 653.

[95] Berutti, *Institutiones,* III, 349; Schäfer, *De Religiosis,* p. 770.

[96] Berutti, *loc. cit.;* Schäfer, *De Religiosis,* p. 770; Coronata, *Institutiones,* I, 876.

of the scandal or the injury and of the moral imputability of the act of the religious who is to be dismissed are to be gathered. The religious is to be heard, if possible, by the superior or his delegate. The major superior with the definitive vote of his council then decides whether the religious is to be dismissed immediately.[97] If there is danger in delay and the major superior cannot be reached, then the local superior is competent to determine the dismissal provided he has the consent of his council as well as that of the local ordinary. The religious then has the obligation to put aside the religious habit.

The next step according to canon 653 is to transfer the entire matter to the Holy See without delay. Berutti [98] maintains that even in such cases wherein a religious of an institute of diocesan approval is involved the local ordinary has no power to settle the case, but must refer the matter to the judgment of the Holy See. However, it seems to be the better opinion to hold that, since the local ordinary possesses the power to give a definitive decree of dismissal in cases concerning members of institutes of diocesan approval,[99] he also, even in the extraordinary cases envisioned in canon 653, possesses the same power to resolve the case through a decree of dismissal.[100]

---

[97] Canon 653.

[98] *Institutiones,* III, 350.

[99] Canons 647; 650, § 2, n. 1; 652, § 1.

[100] Schäfer, *De Religiosis,* p. 779; Wernz-Vidal, *Ius Canonicum,* III, 490, nota 13; Tabera, "Studia Canonica"—*CpR,* XIV (1933), 57.

CHAPTER XIII

ADMINISTRATION OF TEMPORAL GOODS

ARTICLE 1. ADMINISTRATION

The Code grants to religious institutes the right to acquire and to possess temporal goods, subject only to the restrictions and limitations contained in the constitutions of the religious institute.[1] Property acquired by the institute, province or house is subject to the supreme authority of the Apostolic See,[2] inasmuch as the Roman Pontiff is the supreme administrator and dispenser of all ecclesiastical property.[3] To the local ordinary within the confines of his territory has been given the duty to watch carefully over the administration of all ecclesiastical property which has not been exempted from his jurisdiction.[4]

The administration of property belonging to religious institutes of diocesan approval is a right belonging to the superiors and proper officials of the institute. This right is to be exercised according to the canons of the Code and the particular prescriptions of the constitutions of each individual institute.[5] In general, the Code does not concern itself with the details of such administration, except when the valid or licit performance of some act of administration requires the intervention of an authority external to the institute.[6] This chapter will therefore deal with those instances in the law in which the intervention of the local ordinary

---

[1] Canon 531.

[2] Canon 1499, § 2.

[3] Canon 1518.

[4] Canon 1519, § 1.

[5] Canon 532, §§ 1 and 2.

[6] Larraona, "Commentarium Codicis"—*CpR,* XII (1931), 356, nota 481; McManus, *The Administration of Temporal Goods in Religious Institutes,* The Catholic University of America Canon Law Studies, n. 109 (Washington, D. C.: The Catholic University of America, 1937), p. 83.

is necessary for the proper administration of property belonging to a religious institute, together with the nature and extent of the local ordinary's right of vigilance over such property.

Article 2. Investments

Investment is an act of administration by which money is exchanged for goods which will endure and will produce revenue and fruits. These goods may be in the form of real estate, stocks and bonds, or other securities.[7]

Canon 533 gives the regulations which must be followed in the investment of money. In the first place the particular norms of each institute must be carefully observed.[8] If the constitutions, for example, contain provisions which require the consent of the local ordinary for all investments of money, such provisions must be fully adhered to. In the event that no special provision is made, then the consent of the local ordinary is required as outlined below.

Superioresses of congregations of diocesan approval must have the permission of the local ordinary for every investment of money.[9] There arises then the question regarding the meaning of the term "superioress" as employed in canon 533. Does it include the superioress general and the provincial, or only the local superioress?

Larraona [10] seems to be the only commentator who restricts the term to local superioresses, at least when the institute extends beyond the limits of the one diocese. The term itself is used elsewhere in the Code [11] in designation of a superioress other than the local superioress. The two arguments that Larraona presents

---

[7] Larraona, "Commentarium Codicis"—*CpR*, XII (1931), 437; Coronata, *Institutiones*, I, 693. Coronata (*loc. cit.*) notes that money deposited in a bank and subject to withdrawal is not in the canonical sense of the term an investment, even though it is productive of income and was deposited in the bank for that purpose. Such would be only a temporary investment.

[8] Canon 533, § 1.

[9] Canon 533, § 1, n. 1.

[10] "Commentarium Codicis"—*CpR*, XII (1931), 440–441.

[11] Canon 550.

for excluding major superioresses in congregations that extend into more than one diocese are the following.

The first reason is that the general government of such congregations, both as regards economic affairs and in reference to disciplinary matters, does not pertain directly and exclusively to the local ordinary of the diocese in which the mother house is located, unless in particular cases the law specially grants such a right to the local ordinary. The second reason is that, since the local ordinary is given the right to a financial accounting from such institutes only in two instances, namely with respect to the investment of dowries and the administration of the goods of religious houses within his diocese,[12] it does not seem logical to give him a measure of control over investments for the entire congregation and yet deprive him of the means necessary to see the obligation of such a prescription is met.

The better opinion, however, seems to be that which includes all religious superioresses, so that all must obtain the consent of the local ordinary before investing any of the funds of the institute. The terminology of canon 533 [13] seems too extensive and all inclusive to permit a restrictive interpretation.

The consent of the local ordinary must also be obtained by the superior or superioress for the investment of money that represents a fund given or bequeathed to a religious house to be spent locally for divine worship or charity.[14] The obligation of obtaining the consent of the local ordinary rests upon the local superior. Since this prescription refers only to superiors of religious houses and to funds given or bequeathed to religious houses for the purposes indicated above, it is to be deduced that funds given to the province or the congregation itself do not fall under the prescriptions of this canon.[15]

---

[12] Canon 535, § 2 and § 2, n. 1.

[13] Canon 533, § 1: "Sed praevium consensum Ordinarii loci obtinere tenentur:

n. 1. Antistita . . . religionis iuris dioecesani pro cuiusvis pecuniae collocatione."

[14] Canon 533, § 1, n. 3.

[15] Larraona, "Commentarium Codicis"—*CpR,* XIII (1932), 32; Blat, *Commentarium,* III, n. 258; Fanfani, *De Iure Religiosorum,* p. 173; Coronata, *Institutiones,* I, 674, nota 4.

Schäfer, while admitting that intrinsically in relation to his office no local ordinary has a right over the investment of funds given to a province, indicates that such a right can be established through an application of the norms that look to an analogy in the law, as canon 20 intimates.[16] It is clear, however, that the Constitution *Conditae a Christo,*[17] on which this legislation is based, had reference only to funds given to a determined house, to the exclusion of the institute. As to the argument from analogy, it seems more accurate to advert to the analogy, not as it exists between the province and the religious house, but rather as it obtains between the province and the institute itself, since the province is similar in structure to the latter both as to office and power. This is especially the case when the province extends beyond the limits of any one diocese.[18]

The opinion [19] that, since such funds will be spent through a local house, even though given to a province or the institute, their investment should be subjected to the control of the local ordinary, does not seem to be in accord with the prescription of canon 533 and the interpretation given it by commentators. The determining factor here is not alone a question of who will spend the funds, rather it must also be determined to whom the funds were given or bequeathed. Was it the religious house to which they were given, or was it the province or institute itself? The terminology of the canon together with the interpretation of the canonists [20] restricts the case to funds given to the religious house, and the duty of obtaining the necessary consent to the superior of the religious house, so that there seems no justification for extending its meaning.

---

[16] Schäfer, *De Religiosis,* p. 331. While Schäfer does not develop this argument, he seems to contemplate the analogy in the law as between the province and the religious house.

[17] § II, n. IX,—*Fontes,* n. 644.

[18] Larraona, *ibid.,* p. 32, nota 556.

[19] Farrell, *The Rights and Duties of the Local Ordinary Regarding Women Religious of Pontifical Approval,* p. 147.

[20] Larraona, "Commentarium Codicis"—*CpR,* XIII (1932), 31; Vermeersch-Creusen, *Epitome,* I, 341; Schäfer, *De Religiosis,* p. 330; Coronata, *Institutiones,* I, 694; Wernz-Vidal, *Ius Canonicum,* III, 174.

For a proper understanding of the prescription of this canon it is necessary to understand also the meaning of the word " funds " as used here. It does not include donations or legacies given to be spent at once.[21] Included in the term " funds " are not only land and other immovable goods, but also movable goods and money.[22]

Blat[23] maintains that only pious foundations are included in the term " funds," and thus any funds which are not destined to be invested for a sufficiently long period of time to constitute them as a foundation would not fall under the prescriptions of this canon. The term " funds " seems however to be a more general term than foundation, and since the purpose of this prescription is to safeguard investments no matter how long such investments are to remain intact, it seems that the term " funds " here includes all temporal goods, if given or bequeathed with the intention that they be invested, even though only for a determined period of time.

The next condition which must be fulfilled if the prescription of canon 533 is to become operative is that the funds be such as are given to be used locally (in that very place—*eo ipso loco*). Commentators differ on the extent and meaning of this phrase. Schäfer,[24] Vermeersch-Creusen[25] and De Meester[26] extend this term in a way that lets it envision the entire diocese, so that funds given to be expended anywhere in the diocese, no matter what be the extent of the diocese, would be subject to the approval of the local ordinary for their investment. Coronata,[27] Wernz-Vidal[28] and Larraona[29] restrict its meaning to the village, the town, or the city in which the religious house is located.

---

[21] Blat, *Commentarium,* III, n. 258.

[22] Larraona, " Commentarium Codicis "—*CpR,* XIII (1932), 31; Coronata, *Institutiones,* I, 694, nota 5.

[23] *Commentarium,* III, n. 258, 3; Berutti holds the same opinion; cf. *Institutiones,* III, 117.

[24] *De Religiosis,* p. 331.

[25] *Epitome,* I, 341.

[26] *Iuris Canonici et Iuris Canonico-Civilis Compendium* (3 vols. in 4, Brugis, 1921–1928), II, n. 980 (hereafter cited *Compendium*).

[27] *Institutiones,* I, 694, nota 7.

[28] *Ius Canonicum,* III, 181.

[29] " Commentarium Codicis "—*CpR,* XIII (1932), 34.

Larraona gives cogent reasons for his view. He admits that the term *locus* in canon law is used in designation of the limits of the diocese, for example, in the term "ordinary of the place," and again in canon 1516, § 3, where it is expressly so used (*loci seu dioecesis*). Arguing however from the context, he thinks that the use of the two modifiers *eo ipso* appears to be an allusion to a place already at least implicitly designated, that is, the place in which is located the particular religious house whose superior is bound by the prescription.

This argument is supported by a consideration of the source of this prescription, namely the Constitution *Conditae a Christo,*[30] wherein the phrase *eo ipso loco* seems to indicate the very place where the particular house is located. The ordinary meaning of the term "place," especially in reference to domicile, religious houses, pious works and foundations, is that territory which is contained within the limits of a city, town or village, namely the lowest immediate territorial division within which is contained the thing or work concerned. In view of these arguments of Larraona together with the authority of Coronata and Wernz-Vidal, the better interpretation of the term "place" in this context seems to be that which limits it to the city, town or village within which is located the religious house to which the funds have been given.

Canon 533, § 1, n. 3, affects only the investment of funds given or bequeathed either for the worship of God or for charitable works. Worship of God includes Masses offered in the church, the preservation of the church, and the purchase of vestments.[31] Charity includes principally the corporal works of mercy, burses for students, payment of teachers' salaries, and the like.[32] It also seems possible to include under the term "charity" spiritual works, which are not properly ecclesiastical functions, and thus are not included in the term "worship of God." Such for example would be the work of catechizing.[33]

---

[30] § II, n. IX—"Qui vero fundi certae domui tributi legative sint ad Dei cultum beneficentiamve eo ipso loco impendendam: horum administratio moderator quidem domus gerat, referat tamen ad Episcopum, eique se omnino praebeat obnoxium."—*Fontes,* n. 644.

[31] Larraona, *ibid.,* p. 33.

[32] Vermeersch-Creusen, *Epitome,* I, 341.

[33] Larraona, "Commentarium Codicis"—*CpR,* XIII (1932), 33. Larraona

Canon 533, § 1, n. 4,[34] indicates a further instance when the local ordinary's previous permission is required for the investment of money by a religious, namely, when the money has been given to the parish or the mission, or to the religious for the benefit of the parish or the mission. The local ordinary whose consent is required is he in whose diocese the parish or mission in question is located, not the local ordinary of the diocese where the money is to be invested.[35] The term "missions" in general refers to those specific regions which are populated in great part by non-Catholic and pagan peoples, and which are under the care of religious institutes or societies of secular priests. The territories which embrace these missions are known as vicariates or prefectures apostolic.[36] Missions which have their own pastors are called quasi-parishes.[37] By the name parish is understood a distinct territorial part of a diocese, which has its own church, its determined congregation, and its proper pastor.[38]

When therefore money is given for investment to benefit some particular mission, the local ordinary of that mission is to be informed, and the actual definitive investment is to be made only with his approval.[39] If, however, the money is not given to any particular mission but to the missions in general, for example, to the missions of a particular institute, then the entire administration of such funds is the sole duty of the benefitted institute within the framework of its own constitutions.[40]

Unless the contrary is proved, however, anything that is given

---

here notes that goods given to the religious house itself for its own sustenance are not included in this prescript. Cf. also Coronata, *Institutiones,* I, 674, nota 6.

[34] Pro pecuniae quoque collocatione . . . praevium consensum Ordinarii loci obtinere tenentur: . . .

"n. 4 Religiosus quilibet, etsi Ordinis regularis alumnus, si pecunia data sit paroeciae vel missioni, aut religiosis intuitu paroeciae vel missionis."

[35] Schäfer, *De Religiosis,* p. 333; Berutti, *Institutiones,* III, 118.

[36] Canon 216, § 2; Schäfer, *De Religiosis,* p. 332.

[37] Canon 216, § 3.

[38] Canon 216, § 1.

[39] Schäfer, *De Religiosis,* p. 333; Vermeersch-Creusen, *Epitome,* I, 342.

[40] Vermeersch-Creusen, *loc. cit.;* Fanfani, *De Iure Religiosorum,* p. 173; Coronata, *Institutiones,* I, 695; Schäfer, *loc. cit.*

to the rector of a church, be he a religious or a secular, is presumed to be given to the church itself.[41] This is a presumption of the law, but it yields to contrary proof, both direct and indirect, which proof can be derived from the expressed intention of the donor or from other circumstances which clearly indicate the latter's mind and intention.[42] In cases, however, which do not afford any proof to the contrary the presumption remains in favor of the parish or the mission.

The change of the investment of any fund, for the initial investment of which the previous consent of the local ordinary was required, requires his consent anew.[43] This is in keeping with the purpose of the legislation governing the initial investment, namely, the continuous safe and productive investment of these funds. A change of investment does not mean merely the cessation of an investment, but the cessation together with a new investment. The local ordinary's consent is necessary in all such changes, whether the change is made to an entirely different type of investment, for example, from real estate to stocks, or of the same general type, for example, from the stock of one corporation to that of another.[44] The additional consent of the local ordinary is not required for transactions which in reality represent only ordinary acts of administration. Thus the renewal of notes, or the repurchase of bonds under the same conditions when they have matured does not require the consent of the local ordinary.[45]

Article 3. Alienation of Temporal Goods

Alienation in its strict sense is the act by which a physical or

[41] Canon 1536, § 1.

[42] Schäfer, *De Religiosis,* 332; Larraona, "Commentarium Codicis"—*CpR,* XIII (1932), 95–97. Larraona lists circumstances which would indicate that a particular donation was given to the religious or the institute. Thus, for example, the relationship that exists between the religious and the donor, or the occasion of the gift, or its nature, will in some cases give sufficient indication that the gift was intended, not for the parish or the mission, but for the religious, for the religious house, or for the religious institute.

[43] Canon 533, § 2.

[44] Larraona, "Commentarium Codicis"—*CpR,* XIII (1932), 98; Schäfer, *De Religiosis,* p. 333.

[45] Larraona, *loc. cit.;* Schäfer, *loc. cit.*

moral person transfers the direct ownership of ecclesiastical property to another person. This transfer may be made by means of sale, loan, gift, exchange or legacy.[46]

Its meaning in the Code of Canon Law is, however, more extensive and wider, including not only the actual transfer of ownership, but also every act which limits or makes less secure the ownership of ecclesiastical property by transmitting or remitting to another an incorporeal right over the property, as for example in the case of mortgage or lease.[47] It is clear therefore that all contractual debts and obligations which result in a lessening of the financial security of the religious institute, even though no transfer of property or property rights has occurred, are equivalent to alienation and subject to the same rules and restrictions.[48]

Inasmuch as the Church does not as a rule favor alienation of ecclesiastical property, certain requirements have been set up for its licit and valid alienation. There is required, first, a just cause, such as an urgent necessity, a manifest usefulness to the Church, or the promotion of piety.[49] The permission of the legitimate superior must be obtained and without it the alienation would be invalid.[50] A written estimate of the value of the property to be alienated must be obtained from experts in writing[51] and its sale cannot be made for a price less than that set by the experts.[52] It is then required that the sale be a public one or at least that there be a public notice of the intention to sell and, all things considered, that the property be sold to him who offers the best price.[53] The money realized from such alienation must then be

---

[46] Wernz, *Ius Decretalium,* III, n. 157.

[47] Vromant, *De Bonis Ecclesiae Temporalibus ad Usum praesertim Missionariorum et Religiosorum* (Lovanii: Museum Lessianum, 1927), n. 279; Larraona, "Commentarium Codicis"—*CpR,* XIII (1932), 188; Coronata, *Institutiones,* I, 695. McManus, *The Administration of Temporal Goods in Religious Institutes,* pp. 119–120.

[48] Larraona, *loc. cit.;* McManus, *loc. cit.*

[49] Canon 1530, § 1, n. 2.

[50] *Ibid.,* n. 3.

[51] *Ibid.,* n. 1.

[52] Canon 1531, § 1.

[53] Canon 1531, § 2.

placed in a safe and useful investment in accordance with the prescriptions governing the investment of money.[54] If the money received is to be used immediately for some particular work or other purpose, further permission for this must be obtained from the Holy See.[55]

These are the general rules relative to alienation. In applying these to institutes of diocesan approval it is necessary to determine who is the legitimate superior who can give the necessary permission for the valid alienation of the property of religious. In institutes of men religious of diocesan approval, if the property to be alienated does not exceed the sum of six thousand gold dollars, then as a sufficing factor there is required that in accordance with the constitutions the written permission of the proper superior be obtained together with the consent of his council or chapter as revealed upon a secret ballot.[56] The sum is set by the Code at thirty thousand francs or lire, which at the time of the appearance of the Code was approximately six thousand gold dollars. It was the intention to establish a universal norm, applicable everywhere. The norm was based on the gold standard.[57]

This is confirmed by the letter of the Apostolic Delegate to the Ordinaries and religious superiors of the United States.[58] In speaking of the sum of $6,000.00 the Apostolic Delegate noted that it should be "understood in connection with the terms of the Code, as the equivalent of 'thirty thousand lire or francs' and in reference to the value of currency based upon gold in distinction to other currencies, gold being the true unit of value.

---

[54] Canon 1531, § 2.

[55] S. C. C., Dioecesis N., Donarionum Votivorum, 12 iul. 1919—*AAS,* IX (1919), 416; Coronata, *Institutiones,* I, 697.

[56] Canon 534, § 1.

[57] Ellis, "Triginta Millia Libellarum seu Francorum"—*Periodica,* XXVII (1938), 350; Coronata, *Institutiones,* I, 697, nota 4; Wernz-Vidal, *Ius Canonicum,* IV, 230; Schäfer, *De Religiosis,* p. 244; Doheny, *Practical Problems in Church Finance* (Milwaukee, Bruce Publishing Co., 1941), p. 41; Heston, "*The Alienation of Church Property in the United States,* The Catholic University of America Canon Law Studies, n. 132 (Washington, D. C.: The Catholic University of America Press, 1941), p. 112.

[58] 13 nov. 1936—Bouscaren, *The Canon Law Digest* (2 vols., Milwaukee, Bruce Publishing Co., 1934–1943), II, 161-166.

In this connection the value is based upon such stable gold content and rate of exchange." In view therefore of the reduced value of the dollar, which occurred by Presidential proclamation on January 31, 1934, it seems safe to place the present value of thirty thousand lire or francs at approximately ten thousand devaluated dollars. It has been declared safe to follow in practice this manner of computing in dollars the sum which the Code represents in francs or lire.[59]

The permission of the legitimate superior is required for the validity of the alienation,[60] and if this superior should grant his permission without first having obtained the majority vote of his council or chapter he would act invalidly,[61] and the subsequent alienation would likewise be invalid.[62] If the permission of the legitimate superior is given with the consent of the council or chapter, but not in writing, then the permission would be granted illicitly indeed, but validly nevertheless.[63]

In congregations of women religious of diocesan approval, for the alienation of property not exceeding the value of $6,000.00, there is required, besides the validly and licitly granted permission of the superioress, the additional consent of the local ordinary, given in writing.[64] The local ordinary's consent is required for the validity of the alienation.[65] While there is no set minimum value below which the consent of the local ordinary is not required for alienation, an alienation of property of small and insignificant value seems not to require it. Furthermore the constitutions, or the local ordinary in the absence of any such provision in the

---

59 Ellis, *loc. cit.;* Doheny, *loc. cit.;* Heston, *loc. cit.* The sum of $6,000.00 (gold dollars) will be used in the text of this work, but it is to be noted that it admits of the above interpretation.

60 Canon 1530, § 1, n. 3.

61 Canon 105, n. 1; Berutti, *Institutiones,* III, 121.

62 Berutti, *loc. cit.*

63 Berutti, *loc. cit;* Coronata, *Institutiones,* I, 697, nota 6.

64 Canon 534, § 1.

65 Berutti, *Institutiones,* III, 122; Coronata, *Institutiones,* I, 698. The Holy See alone can grant a sanation for an alienation of property invalid due to the failure to obtain the necessary permission from the religious superior or the local ordinary.—Cf. S. C. C., *Albiganen. et Aliarum,* Sanationis Alienationum, 18 maii 1919—*AAS,* XI (1919), 385–386.

constitutions, may specify some specific minimum value below which property may be alienated without his consent.[66]

When the property to be alienated exceeds the sum of $6,000.00, then there is required the additional permission of the Holy See.[67] Failure to receive such permission from the Holy See would render the alienation null and void,[68] but such invalidity could be sanated by the Holy See.[69]

Since debts and obligations are but a form of alienations, in the contracting of them the above noted provisions required for the alienation of property are to be observed,[70] together with the following additional prescriptions. In the petition seeking permission to incur debts and obligations, there must be clearly stated all outstanding debts and obligations of the moral person concerned, that is, of the institute, the province or the religious house, otherwise the granted permission will be invalid.[71] In the petition presented to the Holy See, or now to the Apostolic Delegate, for permission to contract debts or obligations in excess of $6,000.00, there must be contained clear and definite statements on the following facts: [72]

" (1) The *reason* for contracting the debt or assuming the obligation.

---

[66] Creusen-Ellis-Garesché, *Religious Men and Women in the Code,* p. 122.

[67] Canon 534, § 1. The Apostolic Delegate to the United States has been granted faculties by the Sacred Congregation for Religious, " to permit the contraction of loans, sales and alienations of the property belonging to a religious institute, when the sum involved does not exceed a half a million gold dollars, provided that there is observance of the norms which were made known to the Most Reverend Ordinaries and to the religious Superiors by this Apostolic Delegation on November 13, 1936."—Cf. *The Jurist* (Washington, D. C., 1941-), VII (1947), 340.

[68] Canon 534, § 1.

[69] Res. S. C. C., *Albiganen. et Aliarum,* Sanationis Alienationum, 18 maii 1919—*AAS,* XI (1919), 383.

[70] Letter of the Apostolic Delegate addressed to Ordinaries and Religious Superiors of the United States, 13 nov. 1936—Bouscaren, *The Canon Law Digest,* II, 161–166.

[71] Canon 534, § 2.

[72] Letter of the Apostolic Delegate addressed to Ordinaries and Religious Superiors of the United States, 13 nov. 1936.—Bouscaren, *The Canon Law Digest, loc. cit.*

(2) The *nature* of the debt or obligation. A mere general statement does not comply with the requirements for an explicit declaration of intention. For example, a mere statement that permission for a loan is required does not satisfy the requirements if an intention exists to issue bonds or debentures.

(3) The *name* of the person, firm, or corporation with whom the debt or obligation is to be contracted.

(4) The proposed terms of meeting the debt or obligation. This requires a detailed and truthful statement of the arrangements for extinguishing such obligations both as to the interest requirements and the principal debt. This requirement demands a statement of the time contemplated for complete payment. In this regard, attention is called to Canon 536, § 5, which warns superiors not to allow the contracting of debts unless it be certain that the *interest* on them may be met from *current revenue* and that *within a reasonable time* the *capital* may be paid off by means of a lawful amortization fund. For example:

 (a) Loans—the plan of amortization must be presented.

 (b) Annuities—the amounts, the plan of investing the funds and interest arrangement, and plans for meeting annual payment, etc., must be stated in detail.

(5) The *economic condition* of the petitioner, which must be illustrated by the following exhibits:

 (a) A balance sheet of current assets and liabilities. The value of each asset ought to be stated at the current price, not at the purchase or nominal price; e.g., bonds should be listed at the current quotation on the exchange; real estate should be listed according to the tax assessment, depreciation, income, etc.

 (b) A statement of receipts and disbursements over a sufficient period of time to give an accurate estimate of normal receipts and expenditures.

 (c) A separate list of the obligations which do not appear under (a); e.g., obligations as guarantor, surety, trustee, bondsman, etc. This information is required in order to estimate all the certain or con-

> tingent obligations of the petitioner, particularly with reference to the rule regarding coalescence, *supra,* n. III." [73]

This letter of the Apostolic Delegate also draws attention to the fact that the issuance of debenture bonds and their sale in the public market or to private investors, and the system of accepting funds under an annuity agreement providing annuity payments to the donor for life both fall under the provisions of canon 534. Therefore any religious institute, province or house which intends to accept annuities or issue debenture bonds in excess of $6,000.00 must first have a papal indult or the permission of the Apostolic Delegate under the penalty of nullity.[74]

The Sacred Congregation for Religious through this letter of the Apostolic Delegate has also indicated the need for an apostolic indult, when there is a coalescence of the debts or obligations of every kind and nature exceeding the sum of $6,000.00. Thus for example:

"(1) If after having contracted a loan of four thousand dollars, an occasion arises for borrowing a further sum of more than two thousand dollars before payment of the first has been made by the religious—since the total of the financial obligations will exceed six thousand dollars after the second borrowing, it is necessary to have the permission of the Holy See before incurring the second loan.

(2) If a community undertakes several issues of bonds or debentures, each issue being within the limit permitted by the Canon Law, but the total of the issues aggregating a sum exceeding $6,000.00, then an apostolic indult must be obtained.

(3) In the event that a community desires to obtain money by means of *annuities* or life pensions, there will be no need

---

[73] Letter of the Apostolic Delegate addressed to the Ordinaries and Religious Superiors of the United States,—*The Canon Law Digest, loc. cit.*

[74] Letter of the Apostolic Delegate addressed to the Ordinaries and Religious Superiors of the United States, 13 nov. 1936—*The Canon Law Digest,* II, 162–163.

of recourse to the Holy See for a sum up to six thousand dollars; but where the sums aggregate a sum exceeding six thousand dollars, then the community cannot receive any further funds through such annuities without an apostolic indult.

(4) When the amount of *existing* debts or obligations totals four thousand dollars and it is proposed to increase such total indebtedness to more than six thousand dollars, then an apostolic indult is necessary. And such permission is required whether the proposed increase in indebtedness is by contract, mortgage, bond or debenture issue, or any other form which will bring the actual or contingent obligations to a *total sum* of more than six thousand dollars.

(5) When the total *present indebtedness* is over six thousand dollars, an apostolic indult is required for any contract, debt, or other obligation, even if such new indebtedness is incurred for the purpose of complete or partial payment of the preexisting debts or obligations." [75]

In summary it can be stated therefore that religious institutes of diocesan approval, in contracting debts or obligations which exceed $6,000.00, must seek first a papal indult or the permission of the Apostolic Delegate by drawing up the petition in accordance with the instructions indicated in the above quoted letter. In contracting debts or obligations which are not (in themselves or together with existing debts or obligations) in excess of $6,000.00, only congregations of women religious of diocesan approval require the approval of the local ordinary, but this they need under pain of nullity. The norms and rules as set forth in the letter of the Apostolic Delegate could well serve, so it seems, as a method of procedure to be followed by the local ordinary in granting permission for alienation, or for the contracting of debts, to congregations of women religious of diocesan approval.

The written consent of the local ordinary is also required for the renovation of images which are precious because of their age,

---

[75] Letter of the Apostolic Delegate to the Ordinaries and Religious Superiors of the United States, 13 nov. 1936—*The Canon Law Digest,* II, 163–164.

art or veneration, and which have been exposed for the public veneration of the faithful in churches or public oratories. The local ordinary, before granting his consent, must first obtain the advice of prudent experts.[76] Such images cannot be disposed of without the permission of the Holy See.[77]

Article 4. Accounting of Temporal Administration

It is a general principle of canon law [78] that all administrators of ecclesiastical property must render an account of their administration. The persons to whom such an account must be rendered by the administrators of the goods of a religious institute, province or house, are generally determined by the particular constitutions of each institute.[79] In certain specific instances however the Code grants to the local ordinary the right and the duty of receiving a financial accounting from diocesan institutes.

Thus in congregations of women religious an accounting of the administration of the goods which constitute the dowries is to be made to the local ordinary on the occasion of his visitation, and more often if he considers it necessary.[80] His examination should include the dowries of both the novices and the professed.[81] The local ordinary, in fulfilling his obligation in this regard, shall be concerned with the following points: whether or not his permission was obtained for each investment,[82] whether or not the dowry funds of all the professed are properly invested, whether or not the dowry funds of the novices have been kept intact for investment following their profession, and whether or not the funds as they are now invested constitute a safe and fruitful investment.[83] This duty and right belongs to the local ordinary in whose diocese the mother house is located.[84]

---

[76] Canon 1280.

[77] Canon 1281, § 1.

[78] Canon 1525.

[79] Schäfer, *De Religiosis,* p. 343; Coronata, *Institutiones,* I, 679.

[80] Canon 535, § 2.

[81] Larraona, "Commentarium Codicis"—*CpR,* XIV (1933), 350.

[82] Canon 549.

[83] Canon 550.

[84] Coronata, *Institutiones,* I, 706. Cf. *supra,* page 85, for a more detailed consideration of this point.

The local ordinary has a further right to receive a full financial report from each religious house of diocesan approval within his diocese.[85] No distinction is made between men and women religious, so all are equally bound by this prescript. Neither is there any definite time stated for the rendering or the exacting of such an account, so that the local ordinary can demand it whenever and as often as he judges it necessary. Moreover, his demand may affect the entire administration of the goods of the religious house, or extend to only some particular aspect of it.[86]

The method to be used by the local ordinary in exacting such an accounting is not outlined in the Code. Certainly it is within the competence of the local ordinary to inspect periodically the financial books of the religious house in order to obtain a comprehensive view of its financial condition. The local ordinary could make this examination of the financial books of the religious house at regular intervals, for example at the time of visitation. Schäfer [87] and Larraona [88] maintain, however, that it is for the local ordinary to determine the manner in which this accounting is to be made.

It is incumbent upon the local superiors and administrators of temporal goods in the religious house to comply fully with all the pertinent requirements established by the local ordinary. Failure to comply with these requirements, subjects such guilty officers of the religious house to the coercive power of the local ordinary, who is authorized by means of canonical penalties to compel those who are responsible for fulfilling properly the provisions of the Code in this important matter.[89] If, in the investigation of the administration of the temporal goods of a religious house, the local ordinary discovers infractions of the constitutions or of the Code, he is required to correct these by the use of proper measures.[90]

---

[85] Canon 535, § 3, n. 1.

[86] Berutti, *Institutiones,* III, 125.

[87] *De Religiosis,* n. 744.

[88] " Commentarium Codicis "—*CpR,* XIV (1933), 416.

[89] Canon 619; Berutti, *Institutiones,* III, 125.

[90] Larraona, " Commentarium Codicis "—*CpR,* XIV (1933), 348. Larraona points out that the local ordinary could do this by indicating means for the avoidance of unnecessary expenses and the gaining of more profitable investments.

Delinquency of a serious nature, failure to employ proper remedies prescribed in the past, or obvious incompetency would justify the imposition of canonical penalties and even removal from office of the responsible persons.[91]

It remains to determine whether the local ordinary's power extends to an accounting of the financial administration of a province or institute. The language of the Code states that the local ordinary has the right to receive a financial accounting from the religious houses of diocesan approval.[92] In congregations or provinces which are limited to one diocese, the entire congregation or province is under the jurisdiction of the local ordinary. In such cases the local ordinary has the right to an accounting of the financial administration of the institute or province.[93]

However, when the institute or province extends into more than one diocese, can the meaning of this prescription be extended in the case of the mother house to include not only an examination of the financial administration of the religious house itself, but also of the province or the institute? Schäfer,[94] Vermeersch-Creusen [95] and Coronata [96] maintain that the local ordinary seems to possess the right to inquire into and demand an accounting of the financial matters of the institute or province. Their arguments are based on an application of the principles of canon 20, and on the principle of the subjection of religious of diocesan approval to the local ordinary.

The contrary opinion, however, as held by Larraona,[97] is more in accord with the wording of the canon and with the nature of such institutes.[98] This opinion holds that, save in those instances wherein the particular constitutions give the local ordinary more

[91] Larraona, *loc. cit.* After removing an incumbent from office, the local ordinary does not have the right to appoint another in the place of the one removed.

[92] Canon 535, § 3, n. 1.

[93] Larraona, " Commentarium Codicis "—*CpR,* XIV (1933), 418.

[94] *De Religiosis,* p. 250.

[95] *Epitome,* I, 344.

[96] *Institutiones,* I, 700, nota 4.

[97] " Commentarium Codicis "—*CpR,* XIV (1933), 416–418.

[98] Cf. *supra,* Chapter XI on Canonical Visitation, article 3, The Visitation of the Motherhouse, pp. 84–90.

extensive rights, the local ordinary of the diocese in whch the mother house is located has the right to a financial accounting from the religious house exclusively, and not from the province or the institute. The arguments for this view are as follows.

The source of this legislation, the Constitution *Conditae a Christo,*[99] speaks of the bishop as having the right to an accounting of the financial affairs of the religious *house* of such institutes. The canon itself [100] speaks only of the local ordinary's right over the religious house, and in similar cases in the Code the local ordinary's right is specified not as a right over the congregation but simply over the religious house,[101] save in one case, that of canon 533, § 1, n. 1.

In the prescription of this canon no restriction of the obligation is made to the superioress of religious houses; rather, any investment made by any superioress of a religious institute of diocesan approval is subject to the consent of the local ordinary. The wording of this prescription seems to indicate that in those instances in which the Code does use the term "religious house" the intention is precisely to restrict its meaning to include only the house, and not the province or the institute within the scope of the term.[102]

The power of the local ordinary is limited by the boundaries of his diocese, whereas the province and the institute itself transcend diocesan lines. It seems, therefore, that those matters which are common to the institute or province as such, in this case the financial condition and management of the institute or province, are not within the scope of the power of an individual local ordinary to the exclusion of the other local ordinaries in whose dioceses the institute has houses. To claim such exclusive power, the local

---

[99] § I, n. 10—"Dioecesanae cuiusvis sodalitatis domos Episcopus invisendi ius habet, itemque de virtutum studio, de disciplina, de oeconomicis rationibus cognoscendi."—*Fontes,* n. 644.

[100] Canon 535, § 3, "Loci ordinarius ius insuper esto cognoscendi: . . . n. 1. De rationibus oeconomicis domus religiosae iuris dioecesani: . . ."

[101] Thus canon 512, § 1, n. 2, treats of the local ordinary's right to visit individual *houses* of the congregation; canon 533, § 1, n. 3, in the matter of investment, speaks of funds given or bequeathed to a religious *house* as requiring the permission of the local ordinary for investment.

[102] Larraona, "Commentarium Codicis"—*CpR,* XIV (1933), 417.

ordinary should be able to indicate that it is clearly and expressly given to him either in the constitutions of the institute or in the Code itself. The Code does not seem to grant him such power in this case.[102a]

Accordingly it seems proper to state that the necessary viligance that should be exercised over the province and institute in financial matters belongs not exclusively to the local ordinary of the religious house where the general or provincial curia is located, but to all cumulatively in whose dioceses the institute has houses. The interested local ordinaries should therefore make provision whereby a proper and necessary vigilance will be exercised over the financial affairs of institutes of diocesan approval. For example, one (the local ordinary of the mother house) could act as the delegate of the others. A better provision, one which would obviate all ordinary difficulties and insure the regular and systematic checking of the financial condition of the province or the institute, would be to grant in the constitutions this right to the local ordinary of the mother house.

Local ordinaries have also the right to receive an accounting of all the funds given or bequeathed to a religious house for the worship of God and for charity if the funds are destined to be spent locally,[103] as well as those given to a religious for a particular parish or mission. The local ordinary who has the right to this accounting is he whose permission is necessary for the investment of such funds,[104] namely the local ordinary in whose diocese the respective religious house or the parish or mission is located. It is the local ordinary's duty to see that these funds have been properly placed in safe and fruitful investments, and to take any steps necessary, even to the extent of canonical punishments and removal from office, to insure that these funds will be properly administered.[105]

[102a] Cf. note 58 on page 90 concerning the recent decision of the Sacred Congregation of Religious in reference to quinquennial reports to be made by institutes of diocesan approval.

[103] Canon 534, § 3, n. 2.

[104] Canon 533, § 1, nn. 3, 4.

[105] Canon 619; Larraona, "Commentarium Codicis"—*CpR*, XIV (1933), 348.

CONCLUSIONS

1. The mere permission of the Holy See to found a congregation of diocesan approval is not in itself sufficient for the valid, stable and efficient administration of a new congregation. (p. 60)

2. In view of the difficulties met by new congregations at their inception in the application of the laws of the Church, it seems to be proper procedure for the local ordinary to place, together with his request for permission to found a new institute, another request for extraordinary faculties, so that he may properly cope with each of the possible situations that may arise in making such an institute canonically operative. (p. 60)

3. In the matter of the division of a congregation of diocesan approval into provinces, in the absence of provision for such division in the constitutions there is required the consent of each ordinary in whose diocese any of the religious houses are located, together with the consent of the local ordinary of the diocese where the mother house is located. (p. 62)

4. Provided it is not contrary to the original permission of the local ordinary or the will of the donor, a religious house may be transferred within the same city, town or village without a new permission of the local ordinary. (p. 69)

5. The power of the local ordinary over congregations of diocesan approval is one of jurisdiction. (p. 76)

6. The local ordinary, it seems, does not possess the power to break a tie in the election of the superioress general in congregations of diocesan approval. (p. 79)

7. In abstraction from any provisions in the constitutions of the institute, the right of visitation of the entire congregation or province belongs, it seems, not exclusively to the local ordinary of the diocese where the general or provincial curia is located, but to all the local ordinaries collectively in whose dioceses the institute has houses. (p. 90)

8. The local ordinary is obliged to follow the practice of the

Holy See in granting indults of secularization. Thus he is not to grant such indults to religious of diocesan approval in major orders, until they have found a benevolent bishop. (p. 96)

9. The preparatory steps required on the part of the institute of diocesan approval in the dismissal of religious in perpetual vows are not necessary if the local ordinary institutes the action for dismissal. (pp. 104–105)

10. The necessary vigilance that should be exercised over the province and the congregation of diocesan approval in financial matters does not, so it seems, belong to the local ordinary of the diocese where the general or provincial curia is located, but collectively to all local ordinaries in whose dioceses the institute has houses. (pp. 125–126)

BIBLIOGRAPHY

SOURCES

Acta Apostolicae Sedis, Commentarium Officiale, Romae, 1909–

Acta et Decreta Concilii Plenarii Americae Latinae in Urbe Celebrati Anno 1899, Romae, 1902.

Acta et Decreta Sacrorum Conciliorum Recentiorum, Collectio Lacensis, 7 vols., Friburgi Brisgoviae, 1870–1890.

Acta Gregorii Papae XVI, 4 vols., Romae, ex Typographia Polygotta S. C. de Propaganda Fide, 1901–1904.

Acta Sanctae Sedis, 41 vols., Romae, 1865–1908.

Bouscaren, T. L., *The Canon Law Digest,* 2 vols., Milwaukee, The Bruce Publishing Co., 1934–1943.

Bullarum Diplomatum et Privilegiorum Sanctorum Romanorum Pontificum Taurinensis Editio, 25 vols., Augustae Taurinorum, 1857–1872.

Bullarii Romani Continuatio Summorum Pontificum, 14 vols., Prati, 1843-1867.

Canones et Decreta Sacrosancti Oecumenici Concilii Tridentini, Romae, 1904.

Codex Iuris Canonici Pii X Pontificis Maximi iussu digestus Benedicti Papae XV auctoritate promulgatus, praefatione, fontium annotatione et indice analytico-alphabetico ab Emo Petro Card. Gasparri auctus, Romae: Typis Polyglottis Vaticanis, 1917.

Codicis Iuris Canonici Fontes cura Emi Petri Card. Gasparri editi, 9 vols., Romae (later Civitate Vaticana): Typis Polyglottis Vaticanis, 1923-1938. (Vols. VII–IX *ed. cura et studio Emi Iustiniani Card. Serēdi.*)

Collectanea in Usum Secretariae Sacrae Congregationis Episcoporum et Regularium, cura A. Bizzarri Archiepiscopi Phillipensis Secretarii edita, Romae: Ex Typographia Polyglotta, S. C. de Propaganda Fide, 1885.

Corpus Iuris Civilis, Vol. III, *Novellae Constitutiones,* ed. 5. stereotypa, recognovit R. Schoell. Opus Schoelli morte interceptum absolvit G. Kroll, Berolini apud Weidmannos, 1928.

Decretales D. Gregorii Papae IX suae integritati una cum glossis restitutae, Romae, 1582.

Decretum Gratiani emendatum et observationibus illustratum una cum glossis, 2 vols., Romae, 1582.

Jaffé, P., *Regesta Pontificum Romanorum ab condita Ecclesia ad annum post Christum natum MCXCVIII,* editionem secundam correctam et auctam auspiciis G. Wattenbach curaverunt S. Löwenfeld, F. Kaltenbrunner, P. Ewald, 2 vols. in 1, Lipsiae, 1885–1888.

Liber Sextus Decretalium C. Bonifacii Papae VIII, suae integritati cum Clementinis et Extravagantibus, earumque glossis restitutis, Romae, 1582.

Mansi, J., *Sacrorum Conciliorum Nova et Amplissima Collectio,* 53 vols. in 60, Parisiis, Arnhem, Lipsiae, 1901–1927.

Monumenta Germaniae Historica, Leges in 4°, Sectio III (Concilia), Tom. I, ed. F. Maassen, Hanoverae, 1893.

Monumenta Germaniae Historica, Gregorii I Papae registrum epistolarum, Tom. I, pars I, libri i–iv, edidit Paulus Ewald, 1887; Tom. I, pars II, libri v–vii, post Pauli Ewaldi obitum, edidit L. M. Hartmann, 1889; Tom. II, libri viii–xiv, post Pauli Ewaldi obitum, edidit L. M. Hartmann, 1893–1899.

Normae secundum quas S. Cong. Episcoporum et Regularium procedere solet in approbandis Novis Institutis Votorum Simplicium, Romae, Typis S. Cong. de Propaganda Fide, 1901.

Normae secundum quas S. Cong. de Religiosis in novis congregationibus approbandis procedere solet, 6 mart. 1921, Romae, Typis Polyglottis Vaticanis, 1922.

Schroeder, *Disciplinary Decrees of the General Councils,* St. Louis, Mo., B. Herder Co., 1937.

AUTHORS

Augustine, Charles, *A Commentary on the New Code of Canon Law,* 8 vols., St. Louis, Mo., B. Herder Co., Vol. III, 5. ed., 1938.

Bastien, Pierre, *Directoire Canonique a l'Usage des Congregations à Voeux Simples,* 3. ed., Bruges, Beyaert, 1923.

Benedictus XIV, *Institutiones Ecclesiasticae,* Prati, 1844.

Berutti, Christopherus, *Institutiones Iuris Canonici,* 6 vols., Taurini-Romae, Marietti, 1936.

Blat, Albertus, *Commentarium Textus Codicis Iuris Canonici,* 5 vols., Romae, 1919–1927.

Bouix, Dominicus, *Tractatus de Jure Regularium,* 3. ed., 2 vols., Parisiis, 1882–1883.

Bouscaren, T. L.–Ellis, A., *Canon Law, A Text and Commentary,* Milwaukee, The Bruce Publishing Co., 1946.

Chelodi, Joannes, *Ius de Personis iuxta Codicem Iuris Canonici, Praemisso Tractatu de Principiis et Fontibus Iuris Canonici,* ed. altera, a Sac. Ernesto Bertagnolli recognita et aucta, Tridenti, Libr. Edit. Tridentum, 1927.

Claeys Bouuaert, F.–Simenon, G., *Manuale Iuris Canonici,* 3 vols., Gandae et Leodii, apud Auctores, 1930–1931, Vol. I, 3. ed. 1930.

Coronata, Mattheus Conte a, *Institutiones Iuris Canonici ad Usum Utriusque Scholarum,* 2. ed., 5 vols., Taurini, Ex Officina Libraria Marietti, 1939–1947.

Creusen, Joseph–Ellis, Adam–Garesché, Edward, *Religious Men and Women in the Code,* 4. English edition, Milwaukee, The Bruce Publishing Co., 1940.

De Meester, Alphonsus, *Iuris Canonici et Iuris Canonico-Civilis Compendium,* 3 vols. in 4, Brugis, 1921–1928.

Doheny, William, *Practical Problems in Church Finance,* Milwaukee, The Bruce Publishing Co., 1941.

Fanfani, Ludovicus, *De Iure Religiosorum ad Normam Codicis Iuris Canonici,* 2. ed., Taurini-Romae, Ex Officina Libraria Marietti, 1925.

Farrell, B., *The Rights and Duties of the Local Ordinary Regarding Women Religious of Pontifical Approval,* The Catholic University of America Canon Law Studies, n. 128, Washington, D. C., The Catholic University of America Press, 1941.

Ferraris, Lucius, *Prompta Bibliotheca Canonica, Iuridica, Moralis, Theologica necnon Ascetica, Polemica, Rubricistica, et Historica,* 8 vols., Romae 1885–1892; *Supplementum,* ed. Ianuarius Bucceroni, Romae, 1899.

Flanagan, B., *The Canonical Erection of Religious Houses,* The Catholic University of America Canon Law Studies, n. 179, Washington, D. C., The Catholic University of America Press, 1943.

Gallik, G., *The Rights and Duties of Bishops Regarding Diocesan Sisterhoods,* St. Paul, Minn., Wanderer Publishing Co., 1939.

Hefele, J., *Conciliengeschichte,* 9 vols., Freiburg im Br., Herder, Vol. I–VI, 2. ed., 1873–1890; Vols. VII–IX, 1. ed., 1887–1890.

Heimbucher, Max, *Die Orden und Kongregationem der katholischen Kirche,* 3. ed., 2 vols., Paderborn, 1933–1934.

Heston, Edward, *The Alienation of Church Property in the United States,* The Catholic University of America Canon Law Studies, n. 132, Washington, D. C., The Catholic University of America Press, 1941.

Lucidi, Angelus, *De Visitatione Sacrorum Liminum,* 3. ed., 3 vols., ed. Joseph Schneider, Romae, 1883.

Lynch, Timothy, *Contracts between Bishops and Religious Congregations,* Catholic University of America Canon Law Studies, n. 239, Washington, D. C., The Catholic University of America Press, 1946.

Maroto, Ph., *Institutiones Iuris Canonici,* 2 vols., Vol. I., 3. ed., Romae, 1919–1921.

McManus, James, *The Administration of Temporal Goods in Religious Institutes,* The Catholic University of America Canon Law Studies, n. 109, Washington, D. C., The Catholic University of America, 1937.

Michiels, Gommarus, *Principia Generalia de Personis in Ecclesia,* Lublin in Polonia, 1932.

Migne, J. P., *Patrologia Cursus Completus, Series Latina,* 221 vols., Parisiis, 1844–1864.

Montalembert, C. J., *The Monks of the West,* 2 vols., translated by Thomas B. Noonan, Boston, 1872.

Orth, C., *The Approbation of Religious Institutes,* The Catholic University of America Canon Law Studies, n. 71, Washington, D. C., The Catholic University of America, 1931.

Papi, H., *The Government of Religious Communities,* New York, P. J. Kenedy and Sons, 1919.

Parsons, Anscar, *Canonical Elections,* The Catholic University of America Canon Law Studies, n. 118, Washington, D. C., The Catholic University of America Press, 1939.

Pejška, J., *Ius Canonicum Religiosorum,* 3. ed., Friburgi in Brisgovia; Herder, 1927.

Pointek, Cyrillus, *De Indulto Exclaustrationis necnon Saecularizationis,* Green Bay, Wisconsin, 1925.

Raus, J. B., *De Sacrae Obedientiae Virtute et Voto,* 2 vols., Lugduni, Emmanuel Vitte, 1923.

Reilly, T., *The Visitation of Religious,* The Catholic University of America Canon Law Studies, n. 112, Washington, D. C., The Catholic University of America, 1938.

Schäfer, T., *Compendium de Religiosis ad Normam Codicis Iuris Canonici,* Münster in W., Ex Officina Libraria Aschendorff, 1927.

Schmalzgrueber, F., *Ius Ecclesiasticum Universum,* 5 vols. in 12, Romae, 1843–1845.

Suarez, F., *Opera Omnia,* 26 vols., Parisiis, 1856–1861.

Thomassinus, L., *Vetus et Nova Ecclesiae Disciplina circa Beneficia et Beneficiarios,* 3 vols., Venetiis, 1730.

Toso, A., *Ad Codicem Iuris Canonici Commentaria Minora,* 5 vols., Romae, Marietti, 1920–1927.

Van Espen, Z., *Opera Omnia,* 4 vols., Lovanii, 1753.

Vermeersch, A., *De Religiosis Institutis et Personis,* 2 vols., Tom. I, 2. ed., 1907; Tom. II, 4. ed., 1909; *Supplementa et Monumenta,* 4. ed., Bruges, 1909.

Vermeersch, A.,–Creusen, J., *Epitome Iuris Canonici cum Commentariis ad Scholas et ad Usum Privatum,* 3 vols., Vol. I, altera editio, 1924, Mechliniae-Romae, H. Dessain.

Vicente, F., *Recentia Instituta,* Madrid, 1916.

Vromant, G., *De Bonis Ecclesiae Temporalibus ad Usum praesertim Missionariorum et Religiosorum,* Lovanii: Museum Lessianum, 1927.

Wernz, F. X., *Ius Decretalium ad Usum Praelectionum in Scholis Textus Iuris Canonici, sive Iuris Decretalium,* 6 vols., Romae, 1898–1905.

Wernz-F.–Vidal, P., *Ius Canonicum ad Codicis Normam Exactum,* 7 vols. in 8, Romae: Apud Aedes Universitatis Gregorianae, 1923–1938.

ARTICLES

Bizzarri, A., "Annotationes"—*Archiv für katholisches Kirchenrecht,* XV (1866), 412–446.

D'Ambrosio, F., " De Domo Generalitia Instituti Polydioecesani quoad Canonicam Visitationem can. 512, § 1, n. 2 praescriptam et quoad poenas can 2413 sancitas "—*Apollinaris,* I (1928), 417-422.

Ellis, Adam, " Triginta Millia Libellarum seu Francorum "—*Periodica,* XXVII (1938), 348–353.

Ellis, Adam, " The General Chapter of Affairs in a Religious Congregation "—*Review for Religious,* I (1942), 253–258.

Goyeneche, S., " Consultationes "—*CpR,* VI (1925), 86–92; VII (1926), 390–397.

———, " Quaenam sunt attributiones Directoris Congregationis dioecesanae? " —*CpR,* XIV (1933), 351-358.

Larraona, Arcadius, " Annotationes "—*CpRM,* XXI (1940), 133–139.

———, " Commentarium Codicis "—*CpR,* I (1920), 45–50; 133–140; 171–177; V (1924), 41–49; 143–153; 256–269; 324–327; 417–436; VI (1925), 180–186; 324–334; VIII (1927), 22–30; 102–112; 440–448; XII (1931), 353–359; 435–442; XIII (1932), 24–35; 92–99; 184–195; XIV (1933), 345–350; 416–425.

———, " De Visitatorum potestate applicandi poenas in can. 2413 statutas "—*CpR,* X (1929), 368–377.

Maroto, Ph., " Annotationes "—*CpR,* II (1921), 162–168; 322–329; IV (1923); 196–201; V (1924), 122–134.

Tabera, A., " Studia Canonica "—*CpR,* XIII (1932), 115–126; XIV (1933), 53–59.

Vermeersch, A., " Quaesita Varia "—*Periodica,* XII (1923–1924), (1)-(3); (63)-(64).

PERIODICALS

Analecta Ecclesiastica, originally *Analecta Juris Pontificii,* Romae, 1855–1869; Parisiis, 1872–1891; *Analecta Ecclesiastica,* Romae, 1893–1911.

Analecta iuris Pontificii, Romae, 1855–1869; Parisiis, 1872–1891.

Apollinaris, Romae, 1928–

Archiv für katholisches Kirchenrecht, Innsbruck, 1857–1861; Mainz, 1862–

Commentarium pro Religiosis, Romae, 1920–1934; ab anno 1935: *Commentarium pro Religiosis et Missionariis.*

Jurist, The, Washington, D. C., 1941–

Periodica de Re Canonica et Morali utili praesertim Religiosis et Missionariis, Brugis, 1905–1927.

Periodica de Re Morali, Canonica, Liturgica, Brugis, 1928–1936; Romae, 1937–

Review for Religious, St. Mary's, Kansas, 1942–

ABBREVIATIONS

AAS—Acta Apostolicae Sedis.

ASS—Acta Sanctae Sedis.

Bull. Rom. Cont.—Bullarii Romani Continuatio.

Bull. Rom. Taur.—*Bullarium Romanum, ed. Taurensis.*

Coll. Lac.—*Collectio Lacensis.*

CpR—*Commentarium pro Religiosis.*

CpRM—*Commentarium pro Religiosis et Missionariis.*

Fontes—*Codicis Iuris Canonici Fonte, cura Gasparri editi.*

Jaffé,—*Regesta Pontificum Romanorum,* etc. (edited by Ewald, Kaltenbrunner, Löwenfeld).

Mansi—*Sacrorum Conciliorum Nova et Amplissima Collectio.*

MGH—*Monumenta Germaniae Historica.*

MPL—Migne, *Patrologia Latina.*

Periodica—*Periodica de Re Canonica et Morali utili praesertim Religiosis et Missionariis,* 1905–1927; *Periodica de Re Morali, Canonica, Liturgica,* 1928–

P. C. I.—Pontificia Commissio Interpretationis.

S. C. C.—Sacra Congregatio Concilii.

S. C. de Religiosis—Sacra Congregatio de Religiosis.

S. C. Ep. et Reg.—Sacra Congregatio Episcoporum et Regularium.

ALPHABETICAL INDEX

BIOGRAPHICAL NOTE

Stephen Quinn was born in Buffalo, New York, on July 22, 1917. He received his elementary education at Nativity of the Blessed Virgin Mary Parochial School, Buffalo, New York, and was graduated in June, 1931. In September of the same year he entered the minor seminary of the Diocese of Buffalo, The Little Seminary of St. Joseph and the Little Flower, Buffalo, New York, and completed the high school course of study in June, 1935. He then entered the Novitiate of the Missionary Servants of the Most Holy Trinity at Holy Trinity, Alabama, where he made his religious profession on September 8, 1936. He continued his studies at St. Joseph's College, Holy Trinity, Alabama. From 1938 to 1944 his philosophical and theological studies were made at the Catholic University of America and at the Discalced Carmelite College, Washington, D. C. He was ordained to the priesthood on May 18, 1944. In September, 1945, he entered the School of Canon Law of The Catholic University of America, and received the degree of Bachelor of Canon Law in June, 1946, and the Licentiate Degree in Canon Law in June, 1947.

Canon Law Studies *

1. Freriks, Rev. Celestine A., C.PP.S., J.C.D., Religious Congregations in Their External Relations, 121 pp., 1916.
2. Galliher, Rev. Daniel M., O.P., J.C.D., Canonical Elections, 117 pp., 1917.
3. Borkowski, Rev. Aurelius L., O.F.M., J.C.D., De Confraternitatibus Ecclesiasticis, 136 pp., 1918.
4. Castillo, Rev. Cayo, J.C.D., Disertacion Historico-Canonica sobre la Potestad del Cabildo en Sede Vacante o Impedida del Vicario Capitular, 99 pp., 1919 (1918).
5. Kubelbeck, Rev. William J., S.T.B., J.C.D., The Sacred Penitentiaria and Its Relation to Faculties of Ordinaries and Priests, 129 pp., 1918.
6. Petrovits, Rev. Joseph J. C., S.T.D., J.C.D., The New Church Law on Matrimony, X-461 pp., 1919.
7. Hickey, Rev. John J., S.T.B., J.C.D., Irregularities and Simple Impediments in the New Code of Canon Law, 100 pp., 1920.
8. Klekotka, Rev. Peter J., S.T.B., J.C.D., Diocesan Consultors, 179 pp., 1920.
9. Wanenmacher, Rev. Francis, J.C.D., The Evidence in Ecclesiastical Procedure Affecting the Marriage Bond, 1920 (Printed 1935).
10. Golden, Rev. Henry Francis, J.C.D., Parochial Benefices in the New Code, IV-119 pp., 1921 (Printed 1925).
11. Koudelka, Rev. Charles J., J.C.D., Pastors, Their Rights and Duties According to the New Code of Canon Law, 211 pp., 1921.
12. Melo, Rev. Antonius, O.F.M., J.C.D., De Exemptione Regularium, X-188 pp., 1921.
13. Schaaf, Rev. Valentine Theodore, O.F.M., S.T.B., J.C.D., The Cloister, X-180 pp., 1921.
14. Burke, Rev. Thomas Joseph, S.T.D., J.C.D., Competence in Ecclesiastical Tribunals, IV-117 pp., 1922.
15. Leech, Rev. George Leo, J.C.D., A Comparative Study of the Constitution "Apostolicae Sedis" and the "Codex Juris Canonici," 179 pp., 1922.
16. Motry, Rev. Hubert Louis, S.T.D., J.C.D., Diocesan Faculties According to the Code of Canon Law, II-167 pp., 1922.
17. Murphy, Rev. George Lawrence, J.C.D., Delinquencies and Penalties in the Administration and the Reception of the Sacraments, IV-121 pp., 1923.

* All published numbers are available from the Catholic University of America Press, 621 Michigan Ave., N.E., Washington 17, D. C., except the following numbers: 1-114 inclusive, and numbers 116, 118, 120, 122, 123, 162 and 198.

18. O'Reilly, Rev. John Anthony, S.T.B., J.C.D., Ecclesiastical Sepulture in the New Code of Canon Law, II-129 pp., 1923.
19. Michalicka, Rev. Wenceslas Cyrill, O.S.B., J.C.D., Judicial Procedure in Dismissal of Clerical Exempt Religious, 107 pp., 1923.
20. Dargin, Rev. Edward Vincent, S.T.B., J.C.D., Reserved Cases According to the Code of Canon Law, IV-103 pp., 1924.
21. Godfrey, Rev. John A., S.T.B., J.C.D., The Right of Patronage According to the Code of Canon Law, 153 pp., 1924.
22. Hagedorn, Rev. Francis Edward, J.C.D., General Legislation on Indulgences, II-154 pp., 1924.
23. King, Rev. James Ignatius, J.C.D., The Administration of the Sacraments to Dying Non-Catholics, V-141 pp., 1924.
24. Winslow, Rev. Francis Joseph, M.M., J.C.D., Vicars and Prefects Apostolic, IV-149 pp., 1924.
25. Correa, Rev. Jose Servelion, S.T.L., J.C.D., La Potestad Legislativa de la Iglesia Catolica, IV-127 pp., 1925.
26. Dugan, Rev. Henry Francis, A.M., J.C.D., The Judiciary Department of the Diocesan Curia, 87 pp., 1925.
27. Keller, Rev. Charles Frederick, S.T.B., J.C.D., Mass Stipends, 167 pp., 1925.
28. Paschang, Rev. John Linus, J.C.D., The Sacramentals According to the Code of Canon Law, 129 pp., 1925.
29. Piontek, Rev. Cyrillus, O.F.M., S.T.B., J.C.D., De Indulto Exclaustrationis necnon Saecularizationis, XIII-289 pp., 1925.
30. Kearney, Rev. Richard Joseph, S.T.B., J.C.D., Sponsors at Baptism According to the Code of Canon Law, IV-127 pp., 1925.
31. Bartlett, Rev. Chester Joseph, A.M., LL.B., J.C.D., The Tenure of Parochial Property in the United States of America, V-108 pp., 1926.
32. Kilker, Rev. Adrian Jerome, J.C.D., Extreme Unction, V-425 pp., 1926.
33. McCormick, Rev. Robert Emmett, J.C.D., Confessors of Religious, VIII-266 pp., 1926.
34. Miller, Rev. Newton Thomas, J.C.D., Founded Masses According to the Code of Canon Law, VII-93 pp., 1926.
35. Roelker, Rev. Edward G., S.T.D., J.C.D., Principles of Privilege According to the Code of Canon Law, XI-166 pp., 1926.
36. Bakalarczyk, Rev. Richardus, M.I.C., J.U.D., De Novitiatu, VIII-208 pp., 1927.
37. Pizzuti, Rev. Lawrence, O.F.M., J.U.L., De Parochis Religiosis, 1927. (Not Printed.)
38. Bliley, Rev. Nicholas Martin, O.S.B., J.C.D., Altars According to the Code of Canon Law, XIX-132 pp., 1927.
39. Brown, Mr. Brendan Francis, A.B., LL.M., J.U.D., The Canonical Juristic Personality with Special Reference to its Status in the United States of America, V-212 pp., 1927.

40. CAVANAUGH, REV. WILLIAM THOMAS, C.P., J.U.D., The Reservation of the Blessed Sacrament, VIII-101 pp., 1927.
41. DOHENY, REV. WILLIAM J., C.S.C., A.B., J.U.D., Church Property: Modes of Acquisition, X-118 pp., 1927.
42. FELDHAUS, REV. ALOYSIUS H., C.PP.S., J.C.D., Oratories, IX-141 pp., 1927.
43. KELLY, REV. JAMES PATRICK, A.B., J.C.D., The Jurisdiction of the Simple Confessor, X-208 pp., 1927.
44. NEUBERGER, REV. NICHOLAS J., J.C.D., Canon 6 or the Relation of the Codex Juris Canonici to the Preceding Legislation, V-95 pp., 1927.
45. O'KEEFE, REV. GERALD MICHAEL, J.C.D., Matrimonial Dispensations, Powers of Bishops, Priests, and Confessors, VIII-232 pp., 1927.
46. QUIGLEY, REV. JOSEPH A. M., A.B., J.C.D., Condemned Societies, 139 pp., 1927.
47. ZAPLOTNIK, REV. JOHANNES LEO, J.C.D., De Vicariis Foraneis, X-142 pp., 1927.
48. DUSKIE, REV. JOHN ALOYSIUS, A.B., J.C.D., The Canonical Status of the Orientals in the United States, VIII-196 pp., 1928.
49. HYLAND, REV. FRANCIS EDWARD, J.C.D., Excommunication, Its Nature, Historical Development and Effects, VIII-181 pp., 1928.
50. REINMANN, REV. GERALD JOSEPH, O.M.C., J.C.D., The Third Order Secular of Saint Francis, 201 pp., 1928.
51. SCHENK, REV. FRANCIS J., J.C.D., The Matrimonial Impediments of Mixed Religion and Disparity of Cult, XVI-318 pp., 1929.
52. COADY, REV. JOHN JOSEPH, S.T.D., J.U.D., A.M., The Appointment of Pastors, VIII-150 pp., 1929.
53. KAY, REV. THOMAS HENRY, J.C.D., Competence in Matrimonial Procedure, VIII-164 pp., 1929.
54. TURNER, REV. SIDNEY JOSEPH, C.P., J.U.D., The Vow of Poverty, XLIX-217 pp., 1929.
55. KEARNEY, REV. RAYMOND A., A.B., S.T.D., J.C.D., The Principles of Delegation, VII-149 pp., 1929.
56. CONRAN, REV. EDWARD JAMES, A.B., J.C.D., The Interdict, V-163 pp., 1930.
57. O'NEILL, REV. WILLIAM H., J.C.D., Papal Rescripts of Favor, VII-218 pp., 1930.
58. BASTNAGEL, REV. CLEMENT VINCENT, J.U.D., The Appointment of Parochial Adjutants and Assistants, XV-257 pp., 1930.
59. FERRY, REV. WILLIAM A., A.B., J.C.D., Stole Fees, V-136 pp., 1930.
60. COSTELLO, REV. JOHN MICHAEL, A.B., J.C.D., Domicile and Quasi-Domicile, VII-201 pp., 1930.
61. KREMER, REV. MICHAEL NICHOLAS, A.B., S.T.B., J.C.D., Church Support in the United States, VI-136 pp., 1930.
62. ANGULO, REV. LUIS, C.M., J.C.D., Legislation de la Iglesia sobre la intencion en la application de la Santa Misa, VII-104 pp., 1931.

63. Frey, Rev. Wolfgang Norbert, O.S.B., A.B., J.C.D., The Act of Religious Profession, VIII-174 pp., 1931.
64. Roberts, Rev. James Brendan, A.B., J.C.D., The Banns of Marriage, XIV-140 pp., 1931.
65. Ryder, Rev. Raymond Aloysius, A.B., J.C.D., Simony, IX-151 pp., 1931.
66. Campagna, Rev. Angelo, Ph.D., J.U.D., Il Vicario Generale del Vescovo, VII-205 pp., 1931.
67. Cox, Rev. Joseph Godfrey, A.B., J.C.D., The Administration of Seminaries, VI-124 pp., 1931.
68. Gregory, Rev. Donald J., J.U.D., The Pauline Privilege, XV-165 pp., 1931.
69. Donohue, Rev. John F., J.C.D., The Impediment of Crime, VII-110 pp., 1931.
70. Dooley, Rev. Eugene A., O.M.I., J.C.D., Church Law on Sacred Relics, IX-143 pp., 1931.
71. Orth, Rev. Clement Raymond, O.M.C., J.C.D., The Approbation of Religious Institutes, 171 pp., 1931.
72. Pernicone, Rev. Joseph M., A.B., J.C.D., The Ecclesiastical Prohibition of Books, XII-267 pp., 1932.
73. Clinton, Rev. Connell, A.B., J.C.D., The Paschal Precept, IX-108 pp., 1932.
74. Donnelly, Rev. Francis B., A.M., S.T.L., J.C.D., The Diocesan Synod, VIII-125 pp., 1932.
75. Torrente, Rev. Camilo, C.M.F., J.C.D., Las Procesiones Sagradas, V-145 pp., 1932.
76. Murphy, Rev. Edwin J., C.PP.S., J.C.D., Suspension Ex Informata Conscientia, XI-122 pp., 1932.
77. MacKenzie, Rev. Eric F., A.M., S.T.L., J.C.D., The Delict of Heresy in its Commission, Penalization, Absolution, VII-124 pp., 1932.
78. Lyons, Rev. Avitus E., S.T.B., J.C.D., The Collegiate Tribunal of First Instance, XI-147 pp., 1932.
79. Connolly, Rev. Thomas A., J.C.D., Appeals, XI-195 pp., 1932.
80. Sangmeister, Rev. Joseph V., A.B., J.C.D., Force and Fear as Precluding Matrimonial Consent, V-211 pp., 1932.
81. Jaeger, Rev. Leo A., A.B., J.C.D., The Administration of Vacant and Quasi-Vacant Episcopal Sees in the United States, IX-229 pp., 1932.
82. Rimlinger, Rev. Herbert T., J.C.D., Error Invalidating Matrimonial Consent, VII-79 pp., 1932.
83. Barrett, Rev. John D. M., S.S., J.C.D., A Comparative Study of the Third Plenary Council of Baltimore and the Code, IX-221 pp., 1932.
84. Carberry, Rev. John J., Ph.D., S.T.D., J.C.D., The Juridical Form of Marriage, X-177 pp., 1934.
85. Dolan, Rev. John L., A.B., J.C.D., The Defensor Vinculi, XII-157 pp., 1934.

86. HANNAN, REV. JEROME D., A.M., S.T.D., LL.B., J.C.D., The Canon Law of Wills, IX-517 pp., 1934.
87. LEMIEUX, REV. DELISE A., A.M., J.C.D., The Sentence in Ecclesiastical Procedure, IX-131 pp., 1934.
88. O'ROURKE, REV. JAMES J., A.B., J.C.D., Parish Registers, VII-109 pp., 1934.
89. TIMLIN, REV. BARTHOLOMEW, O.F.M., A.M., J.C.D., Conditional Matrimonial Consent, X-381 pp., 1934.
90. WAHL, REV. FRANCIS X., A.B., J.C.D., The Matrimonial Impediments of Consanguinity and Affinity, VI-125 pp., 1934.
91. WHITE, REV. ROBERT J., A.B., LL.B., S.T.B., J.C.D., Canonical Ante-Nuptial Promises and the Civil Law, VI-152 pp., 1934.
92. HERRERA, REV. ANTONIO PARRA, O.C.D., J.C.D., Legislacion Ecclesiastica sobra el Ayuno y la Abstinencia, XI-191 pp., 1935.
93. KENNEDY, REV. EDWIN J., J.C.D., The Special Matrimonial Process in Cases of Evident Nullity, X-165 pp., 1935.
94. MANNING, REV. JOHN J., A.B., J.C.D., Presumption of Law in Matrimonial Procedure, XI-111 pp., 1935.
95. MOEDER, REV. JOHN M., J.C.D., The Proper Bishop for Ordination and Dimissorial Letters, VII-135 pp., 1935.
96. O'MARA, REV. WILLIAM A., A.B., J.C.D., Canonical Causes for Matrimonial Dispensations, IX-155 pp., 1935.
97. REILLY. REV. PETER, J.C.D., Residence of Pastors, IX-81 pp., 1935.
98. SMITH, REV. MARINER T., O.P., S.T.Lr., J.C.D., The Penal Law for Religious, VII-169 pp., 1935.
99. WHALEN, REV. DONALD W., A.M., J.C.D., The Value of Testimonial Evidence in Matrimonial Procedure, XIII-297 pp., 1935.
100. CLEARY, REV. JOSEPH F., J.C.D., Canonical Limitations on the Alienation of Church Property, VIII-141 pp., 1936.
101. GLYNN, REV. JOHN C., J.C.D., The Promoter of Justice, XX-337 pp., 1936.
102. BRENNAN, REV. JAMES H., S.S., M.A., S.T.B., J.C.D., The Simple Convalidation of Marriage, VI-135 pp., 1937.
103. BRUNINI, REV. JOSEPH BERNARD, J.C.D., The Clerical Obligations of Canons 139 and 142, X-121 pp., 1937.
104. CONNOR, REV. MAURICE, A.B., J.C.D., The Administrative Removal of Pastors, VIII-159 pp., 1937.
105. GUILFOYLE, REV. MERLIN JOSEPH, J.C.D., Custom, XI-144 pp., 1937.
106. HUGHES, REV. JAMES AUSTIN, A.B., A.M., J.C.D., Witnesses in Criminal Trials of Clerics, IX-140 pp., 1937.
107. JANSEN, REV. RAYMOND J., A.B., S.T.L., J.C.D., Canonical Provisions for Catechetical Instruction, VII-153 pp., 1937.
108. KEALY, REV. JOHN JAMES, A.B., J.C.D., The Introductory Libellus in Church Court Procedure, XI-121 pp., 1937.

109. McManus, Rev. James Edward, C.SS.R., J.C.D., The Administration of Temporal Goods in Religious Institutes, XVI-196 pp., 1937.
110. Moriarty, Rev. Eugene James, J.C.D., Oaths in Ecclesiastical Courts, X-115 pp., 1937.
111. Rainer, Rev. Eligius George, C.SS.R., J.C.D., Suspension of Clerics, XVII-249 pp., 1937.
112. Reilly, Rev. Thomas F., C.SS.R., J.C.D., Visitation of Religious, VI-195 pp., 1938.
113. Moriarity, Rev. Francis E., C.SS.R., J.C.D., The Extraordinary Absolution from Censures, XV-334 pp., 1938.
114. Connolly, Rev. Nicholas P., J.C.D., The Canonical Erection of Parishes, X-132 pp., 1938.
115. Donovan, Rev. James Joseph, J.C.D., The Pastor's Obligation in Prenuptial Investigation, XII-322 pp., 1938.
116. Harrigan, Rev. Robert J., M.A., S.T.B., J.C.D., The Radical Sanation of Invalid Marriages, VIII-208 pp., 1938.
117. Boffa, Rev. Conrad Humbert, J.C.D., Canonical Provisions for Catholic Schools, VII-211 pp., 1939.
118. Parsons, Rev. Anscar John, O.M.Cap., J.C.D., Canonical Elections, XII-236 pp., 1939.
119. Reilly, Rev. Edward Michael, A.B., J.C.D., The General Norms of Dispensation, XII-156 pp., 1939.
120. Ryan, Rev. Gerald Aloysius, A.B., J.C.D., Principles of Episcopal Jurisdiction, XII-172 pp., 1939.
121. Burton, Rev. Francis James, C.S.C., A.B., J.C.D., A Commentary on Canon 1125, X-222 pp., 1940.
122. Miaskiewicz, Rev. Francis Sigismund, J.C.D., Supplied Jurisdiction According to Canon 209, XII-340 pp., 1940.
123. Rice, Rev. Patrick William, A.B., J.C.D., Proof of Death in Prenuptial Investigation, VIII-156 pp., 1940.
124. Anglin, Rev. Thomas Francis, M.S., J.C.D., The Eucharistic Fast, VIII-183 pp., 1941.
125. Coleman, Rev. John Jerome, J.C.D., The Minister of Confirmation, VI-153 pp., 1941.
126. Downs, Rev. John Emmanuel, A.B., J.C.D., The Concept of Clerical Immunity, XI-163 pp., 1941.
127. Esswein, Rev. Anthony Albert, J.C.D., Extrajudicial Penal Powers of Ecclesiastical Superiors, X-144 pp., 1941.
128. Farrell, Rev. Benjamin Francis, M.A., S.T.L., J.C.D., The Rights and Duties of the Local Ordinary Regarding Congregations of Women Religious of Pontifical Approval, V-195 pp., 1941.
129. Feeney, Rev. Thomas John, A.B., S.T.L., J.C.D., Restitutio in Integrum, VI-169 pp., 1941.
130. Findlay, Rev. Stephen William, O.S.B., A.B., J.C.D., Canonical

Norms Governing the Deposition and Degradation of Clerics, XVII-279 pp., 1941.

131. GOODWINE, REV. JOHN, A.B., S.T.L., J.C.D., The Right of the Church to Acquire Property, VIII-119 pp., 1941.
132. HESTON, REV. EDWARD LOUIS, C.S.C., Ph.D., S.T.D., J.C.D., The Alienation of Church Property in the United States, XII-222 pp., 1941.
133. HOGAN, REV. JAMES JOHN, A.B., S.T.L., J.C.D., Judicial Advocates and Procurators, XIII-200 pp., 1941.
134. KEALY, REV. THOMAS M., A.B., Litt.B., J.C.D., Dowry of Women Religious, IX-152 pp., 1941.
135. KEENE, REV. MICHAEL JAMES, O.S.B., J.C.D., Religious Ordinaries and Canon 198, V-164 pp., 1942.
136. KERIN, REV. CHARLES A., S.S., M.A., S.T.B., J.C.D., The Privation of Christian Burial, XVI-279 pp., 1941.
137. LOUIS, REV. WILLIAM FRANCIS, M.A., J.C.D., Diocesan Archives, X-101 pp., 1941.
138. MCDEVITT, REV. GILBERT JOSEPH, A.B., J.C.D., Legitimacy and Legitimation, X-247 pp., 1941.
139. MCDONOUGH, REV. THOMAS JOSEPH, A.B., J.C.D., Apostolic Administrators, X-217 pp., 1941.
140. MEIER, REV. CARL ANTHONY, A.B., J.C.D., Penal Administrative Procedure Against Negligent Pastors, XI-240 pp., 1941.
141. SCHMIDT, REV. JOHN ROGG, A.B., J.C.D., The Principles of Authentic Interpretation in Canon 17 of the Code of Canon Law, XII-331 pp., 1941.
142. SLAFKOSKY, REV. ANDREW LEONARD, A.B., J.C.D., The Canonical Episcopal Visitation of the Diocese, X-197 pp., 1941.
143. SWOBODA, REV. INNOCENT ROBERT, O.F.M., J.C.D., Ignorance in Relation to the Imputability of Delicts, IX-271 pp., 1941.
144. DUBÉ, REV. ARTHUR JOSEPH, A.B., J.C.D., The General Principles for the Reckoning of Time in Canon Law, VIII-299 pp., 1941.
145. MCBRIDE, REV. JAMES T., A.B., J.C.D., Incardination and Excardination of Seculars, XX-585 pp., 1941.
146 KRÓL, REV. JOHN T., J.C.D., The Defendant in Ecclesiastical Trials, XII-207 pp., 1942.
147. COMYNS, REV. JOSEPH J., C.SS.R., A.B., J.C.D., Papal and Episcopal Administration of Church Property, XIV-155 pp., 1942.
148. BARRY, REV. GARRETT FRANCIS, O.M.I., J.C.D., Violation of the Cloister, XII-260 pp., 1942.
149. BOLDUC, REV. GATIEN, C.S.V., A.B., S.T.L., J.C.D., Les Études dans les Religions Cléricales, VIII-155 pp., 1942.
150. BOYLE, REV. DAVID JOHN, M.A., J.C.D., The Juridic Effects of Moral Certitude on Pre-Nuptial Guarantees, XII-188 pp., 1942.
151. CANAVAN, REV. WALTER JOSEPH, M.A., Litt.D., J.C.D., The Profession of Faith, XII-143 pp., 1942.

152. Desrochers, Rev. Bruno, A.B., Ph.L., S.T.B., J.C.D., Le Premier Concile Plénier de Québéc et le Code de Droit Canonique, XIV–186 pp., 1942.
153. Dillon, Rev. Robert Edward, A.B., J.C.D., Common Law Marriage, X-148 pp., 1942.
154. Dodwell, Rev. Edward John, Ph.D., S.T.B., J.C.D., The Time and Place for the Celebration of Marriage, X-156 pp., 1942.
155. Donnellan, Rev. Thomas Andrew, A.B., J.C.D., The Obligation of the Missa pro Populo, VII-131 pp., 1942.
156. Eltz, Rev. Louis Anthony, A.B., J.C.D., Cooperation in Crime, XII-208 pp., 1942.
157. Gass, Rev. Sylvester Francis, M.A., J.C.D., Ecclesiastical Pensions, XI-206 pp., 1942.
158. Guiniven, Rev. John Joseph, C.SS.R., J.C.D., The Precept of Hearing Mass, XIV-188 pp., 1942.
159. Gluczynski, Rev. John Theophilus, J.C.D., The Desecration and Violation of Churches, X-126 pp., 1942.
160. Hammill, Rev. John Leo, M.A., J.C.D., The Obligations of the Traveler According to Canon 14, VIII-204 pp., 1942.
161. Haydt, Rev. John Joseph, A.B., J.C.D., Reserved Benefices, XI-148 pp., 1942.
162. Huser, Rev. Roger John, O.F.M., A.B., J.C.D., The Crime of Abortion in Canon Law, XII-187 pp., 1942.
163. Kearney, Rev. Francis Patrick, A.B., S.T.L., J.C.D., The Principles of Canon 1127, X-162 pp., 1942.
164. Linahen, Rev. Leo James, S.T.L., J.C.D., De Absolutione Complicis In Peccato Turpi, 114 pp., 1942.
165. McCloskey, Rev. Joseph Aloysius, A.B., J.C.D., The Subject of Ecclesiastical Law According to Canon 12, XVII-246 pp., 1942.
166. O'Neill, Rev. Francis Joseph, C.SS.R., J.C.D., The Dismissal of Religious in Temporary Vows, XIII-220 pp., 1942.
167. Prince, Rev. John Edward, A.B., S.T.B., J.C.D., The Diocesan Chancellor, X-136 pp., 1942.
168. Riesner, Rev. Albert Joseph, C.SS.R., J.C.D., Apostates and Fugitives from Religious Institutes, IX-168 pp., 1942.
169. Stenger, Rev. Joseph Bernard, J.C.D., The Mortgaging of Church Property, 186 pp., 1942.
170. Waldron, Rev. Joseph Francis, A.B., J.C.D., The Minister of Baptism, XII-197 pp., 1942.
171. Willett, Rev. Robert Albert, J.C.D., The Probative Value of Documents in Ecclesiastical Trials, X-124 pp., 1942.
172. Woeber, Rev. Edward Martin, M.A., J.C.D., The Interpellations, XII-161 pp., 1942.
173. Benko, Rev. Matthew Aloysius, O.S.B., M.A., J.C.D., The Abbot *Nullius*, XVI-148 pp., 1943.

174. Christ, Rev. Joseph James, M.A., S.T.L., J.C.D., Dispensation from Vindicative Penalties, XIV-285 pp., 1943.
175. Clancy, Rev. Patrick M. J., O.P., A.B., S.T.Lr., J.C.D., The Local Religious Superior, X-229 pp., 1943.
176. Clarke, Rev. Thomas James, J.C.D., Parish Societies, XII-147 pp., 1943.
177. Connolly, Rev. John Patrick, S.T.L., J.C.D., Synodal Examiners and Parish Priest Consultors, X-223 pp., 1943.
178. Drumm, Rev. William Martin, A.B., J.C.D., Hospital Chaplains, XII-175 pp., 1943.
179. Flanagan, Rev. Bernard Joseph, A.B., S.T.L., J.C.D., The Canonical Erection of Religious Houses, X-147 pp., 1943.
180. Kelleher, Rev. Stephen Joseph, A.B., S.T.B., J.C.D., Discussions with Non-Catholics: Canonical Legislation, X-93 pp., 1943.
181. Lewis, Rev. Gordian, C.P., J.C.D., Chapters in Religious Institutes, XII-169 pp., 1943.
182. Marx, Rev. Adolph, J.C.D., The Declaration of Nullity of Marriages Contracted Outside the Church, X-151 pp., 1943.
183. Matulenas, Rev. Raymond Anthony, O.S.B., A.B., J.C.D., Communication, a Source of Privileges, XII-225 pp., 1943.
184. O'Leary, Rev. Charles Gerard, C.SS.R., J.C.D., Religious Dismissed After Perpetual Profession, X-213 pp., 1943.
185. Power, Rev. Cornelius Michael, J.C.D., The Blessing of Cemeteries, XII-231 pp., 1943.
186. Shuhler, Rev. Ralph Vincent, O.S.A., J.C.D., Privileges of Regulars to Absolve and Dispense, XII-195 pp., 1943.
187. Ziolkowski, Rev. Thaddeus Stanislaus, A.B., J.C.D., The Consecration and Blessing of Churches, XII-151 pp., 1943.
188. Heneghan, Rev. John Joseph, S.T.D., J.C.D., The Marriages of Unworthy Catholics: Canons 1065 and 1066, XVI-213 pp., 1944.
189. Carroll, Rev. Coleman Francis, M.A., S.T.L., J.C.L., Charitable Institutions.
190. Ciesluk, Rev. Joseph Edward, Ph.B., S.T.L., J.C.D., National Parishes in the United States, VI-178 pp., 1944.
191. Coburn, Rev. Vincent Paul, A.B., J.C.D., Marriages of Conscience, XII-172 pp., 1944.
192. Connors, Rev. Charles Paul, C.S.Sp., A.B., J.C.D., Extra-Judicial Procurators in the Code of Canon Law, X-94 pp., 1944.
193. Coyle, Rev. Paul Raymond, A.B., J.C.D., Judicial Exceptions, X-142 pp., 1944.
194. Fair, Rev. Bartholomew Francis, A.B., S.T.L., J.C.D., The Impediment of Abduction, XII-122 pp., 1944.
195. Gallagher, Rev. Thomas Raphael, O.P., A.B., S.T.Lr., J.C.D., The Examination of the Qualities of the Ordinand, X-166 pp., 1944.
196. Gannon, Rev. John Mark, S.T.L., J.C.D., The Interstices Required for the Promotion to Orders, XII-100 pp., 1944.

197. **Goldsmith, Rev. J. William, B.C.S., S.T.L., J.C.D., The Competence of Church and State over Marriage—Disputed Points, X-128 pp., 1944.**
198. Goodwine, Rev. Joseph Gerard, A.B., S.T.D., J.C.D., The Reception of Converts, XIV-326 pp., 1944.
199. Kowalski, Rev. Romuald Eugene, O.F.M., A.B., J.C.D., Sustenance of Religious Houses of Regulars, X-174 pp., 1944.
200. McCoy, Rev. Alan Edward, O.F.M., J.C.D., Force and Fear in Relation to Delictual Imputability and Penal Responsibility, XII-160 pp., 1944.
201. McDevitt, Rev. Vincent John, Ph.B., S.T.L., J.C.L., Perjury.
202. Martin, Rev. Thomas Owen, Ph.D., S.T.D., J.C.D., Adverse Possession, Prescription and Limitation of Actions: The Canonical "Praescriptio," XX-208 pp., 1944.
203. Miklosovic, Rev. Paul John, A.B., J.C.L., Attempted Marriages and Their Consequent Juridic Effects.
204. **Mundy, Rev. Thomas Maurice, A.B., S.T.L., J.C.D., The Union of** Parishes, X—164 pp., 1944.
205. O'Dea, Rev. John Coyle, A.B., J.C.D., The Matrimonial Impediment of Nonage, VIII-126 pp., 1944.
206. Olalia, Rev. Alexander Ayson, S.T.L., J.C.D., A Comparative Study of the Christian Constitution of States and the Constitution of the **Philippine Commonwealth, XII—136 pp., 1944.**
207. Poisson, Rev. Pierre-Marie, C.S.C., A.B., Ph.L., Th.L., J.C.L., Droits Patrimoniaux des Maisons et des Églises Religieuses.
208. Stadalnikas, Rev. Casimir Joseph, M.I.C., J.C.D., Reservation of Censures, X-141 pp., 1944.
209. **Sullivan, Rev. Eugene Henry, S.T.L., J.C.D., Proof of the Reception of the Sacraments, X—165 pp., 1944.**
210. Vaughan, Rev. William Edward, J.C.D., Constitutions for Diocesan Courts, X-210 pp., 1944.
211. **Paro, Rev. Gino, S.T.D., J.C.L., The Right of Apostolic Legation.**
212. Balzer, Rev. Ralph Francis, C.P., J.C.D., The Computation of Time in a Canonical Novitiate, X—227 pp., 1945.
213. Dougherty, Rev. John Whelan, A.B., S.T.L., J.C.D., De Inquisitione Speciali, XII—195 pp., 1945.
214. Dziob, Rev. Michael Walter, J.C.D., The Sacred Congregation for the Oriental Church, XII—181 pp., 1945.
215. Eidenschink, Rev. John Albert, O.S.B., B.A., J.C.D, The Election of Bishops in the Letters of Pope Gregory the Great, VII—200 pp., 1945.
216. Gill, Rev. Nicholas, C.P., J.C.D., The Spiritual Prefect in Clerical Religious Houses of Study, X—140 pp., 1945.
217. **Hynes, Rev. Harry Gerard, S.T.L., J.C.D., The Privileges of Cardinals, XII-183 pp., 1945.**
218. **McDevitt, Rev. Gerald Vincent, S.T.L., J.C.D., The Renunciation** of an Ecclesiastical Office, XIV—179 pp., 1945.

219. Manning, Rev. Joseph Leroy, J.C.D., The Free Conferral of Offices, VIII—116 pp., 1945.
220. **Meyer, Rev. Louis G., O.S.B., A.B., S.T.B., J.C.D., Alms-Gathering** by Religious, XII—163 pp., 1945.
221. O'Donnell, Rev. Cletus Francis, M.A., J.C.D., The Marriage of Minors, XII—268 pp., 1945.
222. **Prunskis, Rev. Joseph, J.C.D., Comparative Law, Ecclesiastical and Civil, in Lithuanian Concordat, X—161 pp., 1945.**
223. **Sweeney, Rev. Francis Patrick, C.SS.R., J.C.D., The Reduction of Clerics to the Lay State, X—199 pp., 1945.**
224. Vogelpohl, Rev. Henry John, J.C.D., The Simple Impediments to Holy Orders, XVI—190 pp., 1945.
225. Brockhaus, Rev. Thomas Aquinas, O.S.B., A.B., J.C.D., Religious who Are Known as *Conversi*, X—127 pp., 1945.
226. Griese, Rev. N. Orville, S.T.D., J.C.D., The Marriage Contract and the Procreation of Offspring, XVI-224 pp., 1946.
227. Boudreaux, Rev. Warren Louis, J.C.D., The "*ab acatholicis nati*" of Canon 1099, § 2, XII-110 pp., 1946.
228. Bowe, Rev. Thomas Joseph, A.B., J.C.D., Religious Superioresses, VIII-206 pp., 1946.
229. Diederichs, Rev. Michael Ferdinand, S.C.J., J.C.D., The Jurisdiction of the Latin Ordinaries over their Oriental Subjects, XIV-153 pp., 1946.
230. Dingman, Rev. Maurice John, A.B., S.T.L., J.C.L., The Plaintiff in Contentious Trials.
231. Frison, Rev. Basil, C.M.F., M.Mus., J.C.D., The Retroactivity of Law, X-221 pp., 1946.
232. Galvin, Rev. William Anthony, M.A., J.C.D., The Administrative Transfer of Pastors, XII-288 pp., 1946.
233. Goracy, Rev. Joseph C., J.C.L., The Diriment Matrimonial Impediment of Major Orders.
234. Hale, Rev. Joseph Francis, M.A., S.T.L., J.C.L., The Pastor of Burial.
235. Henry, Rev. Joseph Arthur, A.B., J.C.D., The Mass and Holy Communion: Inter-Ritual Law, XII-138 pp., 1946.
236. Linenberger, Rev. Herbert, C.PP.S., J.C.L., The False Denunciation of an Innocent Confessor.
237. Lowry, Rev. James Martin, A.B., J.C.D., Dispensation from Private Vows, XII-266 pp., 1946.
238. Lynch, Rev. George Edward, A.B., S.T.L., J.C.D., Coadjutors and Auxiliaries of Bishops, X-107 pp., 1947.
239. Lynch, Rev. Timothy, M.S.SS.T., J.C.D., Contracts between Bishops and Religious Congregations, XIV-232 pp., 1946.
240. McClunn, Rev. Justin David, A.B., S.T.L., J.C.D., Administrative Recourse, VII-142 pp., 1946.

241. Lohmuller, Rev. Martin Nicholas, A.B., J.C.D., The Promulgation of Law, XII-140 pp., 1947.
242. McGrath, Rev. James, A.B., J.C.D., The Privilege of the Canon, XII-156 pp., 1946.
243. Marbach, Rev. Joseph Francis, A.B., J.C.D., Marriage Legislation for the Catholics of the Oriental Rites in the United States and Canada, XIV-314 pp., 1946.
244. Shimkus, Rev. Bernard Aloysius, A.B., J.C.L., The Determination and Transfer of Rite.
245. Smith, Rev. Vincent Michael, A.B., S.T.L., J.C.L., Ignorance Affecting Matrimonial Consent.
246. Wachtrle, Rev. Paul Anthony, A.B., J.C.L., The Baptism of the Children of Non-Catholics.
247. Crotty, Rev. Matthew Michael, J.C.D., The Recipient of First Holy Communion, X-142 pp., 1947.
248. Eagleton, Rev. George, J.C.L., The Quinquennial Faculties, Formula IV.
249. Gibbons, Rev. Marion Leo, C.M., J.C.D., Domicile of the Wife Unlawfully Separated from Her Husband, XIV-171 pp., 1947.
250. Kelly, Rev. Bernard Matthew, S.T.L., J.C.D., The Functions Reserved to Pastors, X-150 pp., 1947.
251. Kilcullen, Rev. Thomas John, LL.M., J.C.D., The Collegiate Moral Person as Party Litigant, X-150 pp., 1947.
252. Lafontaine, Rev. Germain Joseph, W.F., J.C.L., Relations Canoniques entre le Missionaire et Ses Superieurs.
253. Lane, Rev. Loras Thomas, J.C.L., Matrimonial Procedure in Ordinary Court of Second Instance.
254. Lover, Rev. James Francis, C.Ss.R., J.C.D., The Master of Novices, X-168 pp., 1947.
255. McNicholas, Rev. Timothy Joseph, J.C.L., The *Septimae Manus* Witness.
256. Marositz, Rev. Joseph John, M.S.C., J.C.D., Obligations and Privileges of Religious Promoted to the Episcopal or Cardinalitial Dignities, XII-180 pp. 1947.
257. Murphy, Rev. Francis Joseph, J.C.D., Legislative Powers of the Provincial Council, XII-158 pp., 1947.
258. O'Brien, Rev. Romaeus William, O.Carm., J.C.D., The Provincial Superior in Religious Orders of Men, X-294 pp., 1947.
259. Pfaller, Rev. Benedict Anthony, O.S.B., J.C.L., *The ipso facto* Effected Dismissal of Religious.
260. Popek, Rev. Alphonse Sylvester, J.C.D., The Rights and Obligations of Metropolitans, XVIII-460 pp., 1947.
261. Ristuccia, Rev. Bernard Joseph, C.M., J.C.L., Quasi-Religious.
262. Sonntag, Rev. Nathaniel Louis, O.F.M.Cap., J.C.D., Censorship of Special Classes of Books, XII-147 pp., 1947.

263. STADLER, REV. JOSEPH NICHOLAS, J.C.L., Frequent Holy Communion.
264. SZAL, REV. IGNATIUS JOSEPH, J.C.L., The Communication of Catholics with Schismatics, XII-217 pp., 1947.
265. WAGNER, REV. URBAN STANLEY, O.F.M.Conv., J.C.D., Parochial Substitute Vicars and Supplying Priests, IX-126 pp., 1947.
266. QUINN, REV. JOSEPH, M.A., J.C.L., Documents Required for the Reception of Orders.
267. BENNINGTON, REV. JAMES CLEMENT, A.B., J.C.L., The Recipient of Confirmation.
268. BLAHER, REV. DAMIAN JOSEPH, O.F.M., A.B., J.C.L., The Ordinary Processes in Causes of Beatification and Canonization.
269. CLUNE, REV. ROBERT BELL, B.A., J.C.L., The Judicial Interrogation of the Parties.
270. COURTEMANCHE, REV. BASIL F., B.A., J.C.L., The Total Simulation of Matrimonial Consent.
271. DLOUHY, REV. MAUR JOHN, O.S.B., A.B., J.C.L., The Ordination of Exempt Religious.
272. DONOVAN, REV. JOHN THOMAS, PH.B., S.T.L., J.C.L., The Clerical Obligations of Canons 138 and 140.
273. FREKING, REV. FREDERICK W., A.B., S.T.B., J.C.L., The Canonical Installation of Pastors.
274. FULTON, REV. THOMAS B., J.C.L., Prenuptial Investigation.
275. GODLEY, REV. JAMES P., J.C.L., The Time and the Place for the Celebration of Mass.
276. KANE, REV. THOMAS A., A.B., B.S., J.C.L., Jurisdiction of Patriarchs until 1439.
277. KENNEDY, REV. ANDREW A., J.C.L., The Annual Pastoral Report to the Local Ordinary.
278 KONRAD, REV. JOSEPH GEORGE, J.C.L., Transfer of Religious.
279. KRESS, REV. ALPHONSE, J.C.L., Contumacy in Ecclesiastical Trials.
280. MCCARTNEY, REV. MARCELLUS ANTHONY, O.F.M., M.A., J.C.L., Faculties of Regular Confessors.
281. MCCASLIN, REV. EDWARD PATRICK, M.A., S.T.L., J.C.L., The Division of Parishes.
282. MCELROY, REV. FRANCIS J., A.B., J.C.L., The Privileges of Bishops.
283. QUINN, REV. STEPHEN, M.S.SS.T., J.C.L., Relation of the Local Ordinary to Religious of Diocesan Approval.
284. SCHNEIDER, REV. EDELHARD LOUIS, S.D.S., M.A., J.C.L., The Status of Secularized Ex-Religious Clerics.
285. THOMPSON, REV. CHESTER J., A.B., J.C.L., The Simple Removal from Office.

www.ingramcontent.com/pod-product-compliance
Lightning Source LLC
LaVergne TN
LVHW050225080826
844660LV00012B/470

* 9 7 8 0 8 1 3 2 2 4 5 9 6 *